AF531779

Coping in Times of Crisis

Books by Liisa Kyle

You Can Change Your Life: A Workbook to Become the Person You Want to Be

Self-Worth Essentials: A Workbook to Understand Yourself, Accept Yourself, Like Yourself, Respect Yourself, Be Confident, Enjoy Yourself, and Love Yourself

Life Levers: Make Small Changes to Create Big Improvements in Your Life

You Can Get It Done: Choose What to Do, Plan, Start, Stay on Track, Overcome Obstacles, and Finish

Get Over It: Overcome Regret, Disappointments, and Past Mistakes

Overcoming Perfectionism: Solutions for Perfectionists

Overcoming Emotional Eating: Coach Yourself to Manage Cravings, Eat Mindfully, and Foster a Healthy Relationship with Food

Making the Most of 2025: A Workbook

Be More Creative: 101 Activities to Unleash and Grow Your Creativity

Making the Most of Your Retirement: Ways to Foster Health, Happiness & Fulfillment at Any Age

Know Yourself Better: Self-Discovery Questions and Activities

Coach Yourself: Self-Coaching Questions and Activities for Self-Discovery and Personal Growth

40 Ways to Enjoy Turning Forty: Make the Most of Your Milestone Birthday to Have the Best Year Ever

50 Ways to Enjoy Turning Fifty: Make the Most of Your Milestone Birthday to Have the Best Year Ever

Making the Most of Your Milestone Birthday: 52 Ways to Have the Best Year Ever

Coping with the Virus Crisis: Ways to Handle Uncertainty and Navigate the New Normal

Coping IN TIMES OF *Crisis*

WAYS TO HANDLE UNCERTAINTY AND NAVIGATE THE UNKNOWN FUTURE

Liisa Kyle, PhD

ALEPH

ALEPH BOOK COMPANY
An independent publishing firm
promoted by ***Rupa Publications India***

Published in 2020 by Shimmer Press

Published in India in 2024
by Aleph Book Company
7/16 Ansari Road, Daryaganj
New Delhi 110 002

Cover illustrations: Shutterstock/Lusya Lukina

ISBN: 978-81-970811-6-3

1 3 5 7 9 10 8 6 4 2

Printed in India

Contents

CHAPTER 1

What is Your Current Situation?

What is kind of crisis you are facing? It might be personal or professional. It could be a health challenge or a financial setback or a combination of multiple major problems. Perhaps there are things going on in the world that are causing or compounding your anxiety.

Whatever the nature of your crisis, you are likely to experience heightened emotions. You may need to manage stress, hopelessness, anger, grief, anxiety, and more. You might be experiencing physical symptoms or ailments as your body bears the strain of your burdens.

Worries and negative thoughts might be foremost in your mind. You could be finding it difficult to concentrate or to get things done. You may be riddled with valid concerns about your well-being and how things will unfold for you.

You might be stuck, unable to take productive action. You may find yourself doing things that aren't helpful or healthy, like over-eating, self-medicating, or obsessing over social media.

The most challenging situations to deal with are those that are out of your control. If there is little you can do to affect what is happening, it can feel like you are at the mercy of the situation and the uncertain future.

However, even if there is nothing you can do to control or affect your current circumstances, there **are** things you can do to change your responses to what is happening. There **are** concrete steps you can take to better cope with your crisis.

I'm writing this book to help you do just that. I'm a PhD in psychology, a life coach, and the author of two dozen self-help books. I've spent the last two decades helping people overcome challenges and manage difficult situations. In 2020, I published a book devoted to helping people cope with the Covid crisis. This book is an updated, more generalized version designed to guide you through whatever crisis you are facing. It provides proven techniques to help you:

- Tend to the basics:
    - Control what you can
    - Suspend self-judgment
    - Address your fundamental human needs: safety and physical, mental, spiritual, and social self-care
- Handle your emotions:
    - Examine and manage your sadness, grief, anger, fear, and anxiety
    - Reduce stress and cultivate calm
- Manage your mind:
    - Cultivate positive thoughts and counter negative thoughts
    - Identify and implement healthy distractions
    - Disrupt negative thinking loops
- Take action and make the best of the situation:
    - Identify opportunities
    - Make desired changes in your life
    - Strengthen important relationships and resolve conflicts and resentments
    - Forgive

- Put things in order:
  - Identify priorities
  - Living space
  - Prune your belongings
  - Finances
  - Legal documents
- Deal with Ongoing or Long-Term Crises
- Navigate the Unknown Future:
  - Examine lessons learned
  - Identify your values
  - Evaluate your priorities
  - Take stock of your personal resources and liabilities
  - Make conscious choices

Please consider this book to be a resource and source of support for you during your crisis. At any given moment, some parts of this book will be more relevant to your situation and challenges than others. Feel free to hop around to whichever sections you need, when you need them. Work through the contents at a pace that is comfortable and engaging for you, in the order that makes sense for you. (Note that there is some repetition woven across the chapters to accommodate this flexibility.)

Each chapter features proven techniques and practical tools. Try them out. See what works for you.

You will get more out of this book if you participate. If the activity involves answering questions, it is more powerful if you actually write (or type) them out. Once you begin jotting down your responses, you will notice that new insights will emerge faster and more clearly than if you simply scan the questions and assume you know how you'll respond. If you really want to learn ways to cope with your current crisis, write out your responses.

◆

HOW ARE YOU REACTING TO YOUR CURRENT CRISIS?

The first step in coping with the current situation is to clarify what exactly, you are experiencing at this time. Different people respond to crises in varying ways. As events unfold and time passes, each person's responses move through different phases. Where are you today?

ACTIVITY

Take stock of your current state. Jot down answers to the following questions:

1. How are you reacting to your current situation?
    - What emotions are you experiencing today?
    - Where in your body do you detect each of these feelings?
    - Are you experiencing any physical symptoms or ailments in response to your current circumstances?
2. What are you thinking? What thoughts are foremost in your mind?
3. How is your self-care? To what extent are you taking good care of your physical, mental, spiritual, and social needs?
4. To what extent are you taking action?
5. To what extent are you making the best of the situation?
6. What is the expected duration of your crisis? Is it something relatively short-term or is it something longer-term or with no end in sight?
7. To what extent are you concerned about the future?

Review your answers to the questions above. What is the greatest challenge for you at this time?

If you are not taking good care of yourself, or if you need to address practical concerns, turn to Chapter 2.

If you are grappling with your emotions, start with Chapter 3.

If you are consumed by unhelpful or negative thoughts, begin with Chapter 4.

If you are having difficulty taking action—if you are avoiding or procrastinating or stuck—go to Chapter 5.

If you are looking for ways to make the best of this situation, turn to Chapter 6.

If you are having trouble dealing with ongoing or long-term challenges, start with Chapter 7.

If you are seeking to prepare yourself for the unknown future, go to Chapter 8.

If you can't decide, begin with the next chapter.

CHAPTER 2

Tend to the Basics

How has your crisis affected your life? Have your regular routines been disrupted? Are you struggling to attend to fundamental tasks? If so, this chapter provides ways you can get back on track.

Are you so caught up in tending to others, you aren't looking after yourself well? If you a "people pleaser" under normal circumstances, you risk becoming a martyr in times of crisis. Remember: if you don't take care of yourself, you can't take care of everyone who depends on you. Put your own oxygen mask on first.

As you deal with your crisis, make sure to address your fundamental human requirements. Establish safety and attend to your physical, mental, spiritual, and social needs. As you do so, you'll begin to establish control, which is an essential way to deal with uncertainty. If you are overwhelmed with what's happening, establish control over something. Anything.

◆

CONTROL WHAT YOU CAN

You cannot control what has happened in the past. You cannot control the events that are unfolding in the present. You cannot control the economy or science or the weather.

What *can* you control? Find something, anything, to take charge of. Consider that you do have control over what you wear, the state of your living space, your activities, your actions, and how you spend your available time.

You could, for example, choose your outfit for the day. You could prepare a nourishing meal. You could call people you care about. You could tidy your living space.

If you are feeling powerless—if you seem to be at the mercy of uncertain circumstances—making deliberate decisions will make you feel better. Taking purposeful actions will give you power.

ACTIVITY

1. Under the current circumstances, what can you control? Make a list. *Please take a few minutes to actually jot down your answers. The point is to demonstrate that you do have some control over some things during your crisis.*
2. What actions can you take today that would be healthy or helpful?

You can't control many aspects of your crisis, but you *can* control how you are spending at least some of your time. Structure can help. Make a daily or weekly schedule to ensure you are tending to your priorities.

Make conscious decisions about what you are doing and not doing. It's fine to spend hours lying on the sofa, watching Netflix—if that is making you happy and if that's what you really want to do. But it's a different thing if you find yourself neglecting your well-being and passing up things you'd rather be doing by passively assuming the role of a couch potato.

Avoid acting like a victim by asserting control over the things you can. Choose what you'd like to do. Be clear about what you don't want to do. It doesn't matter how you decide to spend your time, as long as it is your choice. Even if the circumstances require you to be doing things that you wouldn't choose to do, find some way to manage those tasks in a way that makes you feel as if you have some control.

Maybe you are the only person available to take care of an ill family member. You didn't choose this situation however you have control over how you carry out the tasks at hand. You could be resentful and complaining...or you could be grateful for your own health and the opportunity to help.

If you find yourself in unpleasant circumstances, find ways to make them more palatable. Play music you enjoy. Take breaks. Reward yourself for your efforts. Seek moments of joy, of humor, of beauty in whatever you're going through.

If you find yourself drifting through your days without purpose, pause and ask yourself: how does this feel? If you feel happy and healthy, serenely surrendering to whatever is unfolding, great! Carry on. If, however, you feel icky or guilty or lost or uncomfortable, make a change. Decide how you'd prefer to be spending your time. Set reasonable intentions.

If you'd like, you could choose different priorities for each day of the week. How do you want to spend the free time you have available?

Maybe Monday is "cleaning day" and Tuesday is devoted to reaching out to friends and family members. Wednesday and Thursday might be set aside to work on a big project you've been putting off while Friday's priority could be planning healthy meals for the next week. Saturday might be a Play Day spent enjoying your favorite leisure pursuits and Sunday might be a day of sloth with no expectations whatsoever.

Take control over the things you can—and cut yourself some slack.

◆

SUSPEND SELF-JUDGMENT

During a time of crisis, your brain is likely to be overloaded with processing what is happening, finding solutions to challenges, handling your emotions, and attending to all your personal and work responsibilities.

Be realistic. What can you reasonably expect of yourself, under the current circumstances? How can you set practical expectations for yourself?

Aim to do less. Make your personal coping a priority, then add a few essentials. Focus on small actions. Break larger tasks into baby steps. Seek progress at a reasonable pace.

Know that you may go through phases of needing to coddle yourself. There is nothing wrong with that.

Understand that some days will be more pleasant or productive than others. Count any forward progress as a win.

Avoid judging yourself. You are doing the best you can, under trying circumstances. Be kind, gentle, and forgiving of yourself. Adjust your expectations of yourself.

Similarly, understand that in times of crisis, you may not be acting your "best". You might find yourself lashing out disproportionately over small matters. You may snap at people for no good reason. You might be cranky or weepy or mean.

Suspend judgment. Understand that you are under stress and this is how it's manifesting. Forgive yourself any lapses in grace. Apologize to others when you blurt out something you wish you hadn't, in a tone you regret (as well, you may wish to check out Chapter 3).

Consider your inner dialog. What is the tone of the little voice in your head? To what extent are you nurturing and soothing yourself? If you are operating as your own personal cheerleader, wonderful! Please skip ahead to the next section.

Or do you have an inner critic? Are you judging your actions? Are you berating yourself for what you are doing or not doing?

If you are someone who tends to criticize yourself under normal circumstances, you may find that you are being even harsher with yourself during times of crisis. If that sounds like you, try something new. Going forward, when you notice your inner critic, quell it.

One way to do so is to actually write out whatever your inner critic is saying, then analyze each statement. Is it accurate? Is it valid? What evidence is there to the contrary? Might the opposite be true?

For example, if your inner critic is saying, *"You are being so darn lazy! Why aren't you getting more done?"*, you might counter it with something like:

I'm doing the best I can in a scary, uncertain time. My only interest right now is to get through this crisis as best I can.

If you are aware of self-criticizing thoughts in your head, take a few moments right now to write (or type) what your inner critic is saying—and dispute each statement. Then identify any thoughts you'd prefer to have in your head. For example, instead of *"I am being so darn lazy!"* you may prefer to think:

- *I'm doing what I can. I'm taking care of the basics.*
- *I'm doing the best I can, under the circumstances.*
- *My priority right now is to focus on coping and being kind to myself.*

TECHNIQUE
Quell Your Inner Critic

---

1. What is your inner critic saying? Write down any critical or judgmental statements in your mind.
2. What tone does your inner critic use? Does it sound like anyone from your past?
3. What is your inner critic afraid of?
4. What is the impact of your inner critic on you? How does it make you feel?
5. Dispute what your inner critic is saying. Is it valid? What evidence is there to the contrary? Might the opposite be true?
6. What would you rather believe? Write out thoughts you would rather have in your mind.

Bonus Activity: post your answers to the last somewhere where you will see it often. Read it every day.

It's important to keep your inner critic at bay as you navigate the challenges of your current situation.

◆

ADDRESS YOUR FUNDAMENTAL HUMAN NEEDS

We are complex beings with multiple needs. As we go through a crisis or uncertain times, we sometimes let things slip. If things feel off kilter, it's important to ensure that you are tending to all the basic areas of your life:

- Safety
- Self-care
- Physical

- Mental
- Spiritual
- Social

The remainder of this chapter will cover each of these in turn. Feel free to jump to whichever topics are most important or pressing to you. Please skip over the areas you have well in hand.

◆

MAXIMIZE YOUR SAFETY

Do you have a safe, secure place to live? If so, be grateful and go ahead to the next section.

If not, brainstorm solutions. You cannot cope effectively with your crisis if you can't ensure your basic safety. What can you improve your security? Who can you ask for ideas, help, or support?

If you are feeling too overwhelmed to cope, turn to someone you trust. Call a friend, family member, or neighbor to help you figure out solutions. There are online resources and community groups devoted to providing every kind of assistance.

Note: *if you or your children are experiencing mental, verbal, or physical abuse in your home, you do NOT have to stay in that situation. Please leave and get help. If you don't know how to do so, do an online search for "domestic abuse help [insert your location]". If that's not possible, go to any location in which you feel safer. Is there a fire department, police station, community center, or place of worship nearby? Go.*

◆

PRACTICE GOOD SELF-CARE

To what extent are you taking good care of yourself in your current situation? Take a few minutes to contemplate how you are treating yourself.

ACTIVITY

1. What does good self-care mean to you? When you take good care of yourself, what do you do? Make a list.
2. Review your list. To what extent are you doing these things during your crisis? Which are you doing? Which are you not doing?
3. What adjustments would you like to make? How can you do so?

Often, we signal our level of self-care through our appearance, our grooming, and our attire.

ACTIVITY

Go to a mirror. Look at what you are wearing.

- How well-groomed are you?
- How do your clothes look on you?
- How does your outfit make you feel?

What we wear can have a huge impact on our psyche, our mood, and our self-esteem.

Some people feel great in sweats or daytime pajamas. *So freeing! So comfortable!* Others find it demoralizing. *Omigod, I feel like such a slob!*

If what you are wearing makes you feel good about yourself, wonderful!

If it doesn't, what adjustments could you make to feel better? Do you need to ditch your PJs and put on clothes suitable to wear in public? Would a brighter color lift your spirits?

That's the point of self-care: finding ways to feel good.

It's vital to be kind and gentle with yourself during your current circumstances. This is highly personalized so take a moment to think about how you can treat yourself well.

What are your favorite simple pleasures? What are the little things that give you joy in your life?

What music do you enjoy? What were your favorite tunes in high school? Are there particular meals that make you happy? What are your favorite comfort foods from childhood? Are there little treats you can give yourself to enrich your day? Julia buys herself a fresh bouquet every week. Matt treats himself to comic books (sorry, I mean "graphic novels").

Many simple pleasures don't cost a cent. Keisha's favorite indulgence is to take a nap. Paulo is finding joy in exploring online museum collections. Maria enjoys the videos and comedy bits that celebrities share on social media.

ACTIVITY

1. Think about your best friend. How do they treat you? What could you do to treat yourself more like your best friend?
2. How can you be kind to yourself as you go through your crisis?
3. What simple pleasures do you enjoy?
4. What treats might you give to yourself?
5. What soothes you? How can you soothe yourself?
6. Who soothes you? Who can you turn to for comfort and solace?

Please make a point of doing the following activity today:

> ACTIVITY
>
> 1. What's one nice thing you could do for yourself today?
> 2. Make a point of doing it.
>
> Bonus Activity: repeat this every day.

PHYSICAL NEEDS

1. Practice Good Body Maintenance

How often are you showering or bathing? How is your dental hygiene these days?

During uncertain and stressful times, we sometimes need to remind ourselves about basic self-care. If your regular routine has been disrupted, find ways to re-start it. What are gentle, easy ways for you tonudge yourself to take care of your body?

It's okay, for example, if you need to make a checklist to remind yourself to shower and brush your teeth. It's fine to give yourself stars or checkmarks on your calendar every time you do. Do what you can to get yourself back on track.

Apply the same approach to what you are putting into your body. Are you drinking enough water? It's easy to get dehydrated during stressful times so make a point of drinking water throughout the day.

To what extent are you eating nourishing food? If you've been eating poorly, find ways to fuel your body in healthier ways. Nudge yourself to take better care of your body.

Are you over-using drugs, alcohol, or other substances? Are you stress-eating?

It's understandable if you have turned to these habits to soothe or numb yourself. You are going through a challenging, scary, uncertain time. It's natural to try to reduce your discomfort. There is nothing wrong with short-term self-medication. Don't worry if you have put on a few pounds. You can deal with that as things stabilize.

If, however, these indulgences are prolonged without moderation for long periods of time, they can become problematic and possibly addictive. Consider how you are self-medicating. Are these behaviors actually helping you cope? Do you want to continue doing so? Are you concerned about the level of your current consumption or usage? Consider the impact on yourself and the people around you.

If/when you are ready to curtail your consumption, make a commitment to do so and make a plan:

- How can you curtail the habit you've established? How can you interrupt it? How can you eliminate triggers? How can you limit your behavior?
- How can you address your real needs underlying this behavior? *I'm reaching for a sandwich but am I truly hungry? Maybe I'm thirsty. Is it fear? Am I trying to soothe or comfort myself? Am I wanting to give myself a treat? Am I bored? Do I need something to do? Am I lonely?* Identify your true needs and take action to remedy what's really going on.
- How will you deal with cravings when they occur? Plot a specific course of action. *When I want to stress-eat, I will remind myself why I want to avoid unnecessary calories. I will sip a cup of tea. I will call a friend. I will do five jumping jacks.*
- How might you distract yourself (pp. 78–9)? What might

be other, healthier, more helpful activities you could do instead?

- What support is available to you? Consider people you trust as well as support groups and organizations dedicated to help people overcome your habit. Whatever your vice, there are free virtual meetings and online discussion groups with other people grappling with the same challenge.

2. If You Can Do So Safely, Get Outside

Our bodies are not meant to be cooped up inside all day, every day. Sunshine and fresh air are as vital as food and water. Research shows that when you spend time outside, you have lower blood pressure and better heart rate variability. Getting out into nature is also a proven way to reduce anxiety and improve your mood. Even just five minutes outdoors can give you a boost (more on that in Chapter 3.)

If it is possible for you to go outdoors—if you have a yard or a porch or a balcony or a safe place to walk—make a point of doing so. Every day, if possible.

If you are trapped inside, spend some near a window. Spend a few minutes basking in the sunlight, even if it's through glass. Close your eyes and imagine you are in an outdoor location you find pleasant. Imagine the sights, sounds, smells, and textures in that place.

Or, consider a light therapy lamp. These are inexpensive devices typically used to treat seasonal affective disorder by mimicking exposure to sunlight. Another option might be to replace some of your lights with full spectrum bulbs. Your body will think it is outside and respond by elevating your mood.

3. Move Your Body Every Day

Regular physical activity is essential for everyone. Our bodies crave movement and our brains function better when we do. Physical activity is a proven mood-lifter and stress-buster. During a crisis, it's vital.

If you are disabled, incapacitated, or injured, are you able to stretch or alter the position of your body? What physical activity is possible? To the extent you can move your body comfortably, do so.

If you are able-bodied and live a physically active life, excellent! Please skip ahead to the next section.

If you are able-bodied and not currently very physically active, how can you get your body moving? Do whatever is fun and easy for you.

Do you love gardening or yard work? Do you have access to children or pets you could play with?

As soon as you begin moving your body more, you will start to experience the physical and psychological benefits. It doesn't matter what you do, as long as you are moving your body at least fifteen minutes every day.

If in doubt, walk. Walking is easy, free, and can be done indoors or out. If you can't get outside, walk around inside your home. During the Covid crisis, for example, Justin Denson ran a marathon inside his Colorado condo. In Britain, ninety-nine-year-old veteran Captain Tom Moore set out to raise £1000 for charity by walking one hundred laps around his yard. Pushing his walker, sporting a suit and his military service medals, his efforts went viral and generated over £30 million for the National Health Service.

Physical activity is even more important if you spend most

of your day sitting. Studies have shown that those who do are inadvertently causing their body unnecessary damage. People who sit for eight or more hours a day have the same risk of dying as people who smoke! A sedentary lifestyle slows metabolism and raises blood pressure, blood sugar, and cholesterol levels. It increases the risk of obesity, cardiovascular disease, and cancer.

The good news is that research has also shown that just sixty to seventy-five minutes of daily, moderate physical activities counters the negative effects of being sedentary.

If you are able-bodied, it's vital that you get up and move throughout the day. Make a point of standing when possible. Take stretch breaks. Find ways to move your body. Do what you can. Start with thirty minutes of movement per day. Ideally, work your way up to sixty minutes, seventy-five minutes, or more if you can.

As well, consider what exercise options might be fun for you. If you love to dance, for example, you could take a class or dance along with YouTube videos or download a dance app on your phone.

What might make sense, given your preferences and circumstances? What fitness equipment do you have access to? Do you prefer to work out by yourself or would you prefer a live or virtual class? What options are convenient, given your location and schedule?

Are there apps or devices that would motivate you to be more active? (E.g., pedometers, Fitbits, or training apps.) There are countless free fitness apps, YouTube videos, and online classes available.

Is there a fitness activity you enjoyed in the past that you are no longer doing? Is there something you haven't yet done but would like to try? Maybe yoga or tai chi or Zumba? If you research online offerings, you may discover appealing options that you didn't know existed.

HELPFUL DAILY PRACTICE

Move Your Body

If you are able-bodied and moderately active: make a point of engaging in at least fifteen minutes of physical activity every day. The more, the better.

If you sit most of the day, do more: begin with at least thirty minutes of daily physical activity. Work your way up to at least sixty or seventy-five minutes a day.

If you are injured, incapacitated, or disabled: find an equivalent activity that works for you. Move your body to the extent you can.

---

4. Foster Good Sleep

How is your sleep these days? Are you able to fall asleep easily? Are you waking up in the middle of the night? Are you experiencing unusually vivid dreams? Are you over-sleeping?

Do what you can to foster good sleep. What works well for you? Reading? A warm beverage? A weighted blanket? A fan or white noise machine? Consider turning off your computer or tablet for at least an hour before bedtime. The absence of the screen light signals to your brain and body that it is night and time for sleep.

The worst thing to do when you have trouble sleeping is to start to fret about the fact that you're not sleeping. *"Oh no! I can't sleep! I'll never be able to get to sleep!"* If this sounds like you, the best thing you can do is catch yourself—laugh at yourself if possible—and remind yourself of a few truths: First, yes, a good night's sleep is important and yet you are perfectly able to function on less sleep from time to time. Yes, you'd prefer to be well-rested—but if you aren't, the impact of your sleep-deprived state is not likely to be detectable to anyone else. You might be aware you're not at your best, but others are unlikely to notice anything amiss.

If you should wake up in the middle of the night, there is no need to panic. Did you know that, until about a hundred years ago, people practiced a natural "segmented sleep" pattern: They would sleep for a few hours, then get up in the middle of the night to tend to chores or family matters or pray or even socialize—then return to bed to sleep some more.

Waking up in the middle of the night is not a big deal. It's actually *normal* for us humans. There's no reason to lie in bed, tossing and turning, fretting that you've only slept for a couple hours. Instead, get up for a while. Savor the quiet. Do something pleasant. Read. Stretch your body. Meditate. Work on a hobby. Journal. Play with a puzzle.

Here's one caution, though: if you do wake up in the middle of the night, avoid the temptation to fire up your computer or television or another bright screen. The unnatural light source tricks your body into thinking it is morning already and then (a) you won't get back to sleep and (b) you're messing with your circadian rhythms.

Instead, why not use this 'middle of the night' time as a treat for yourself? You could use it to:

- Indulge in simple pleasures
- Attend to your body (e.g., do some gentle stretching, take a soothing bath)

- Do some personal processing (e.g., write in your journal, make gratitude lists; refer to p. 67)
- Nourish your mind (e.g., read, listen to music, work on puzzles)
- Meditate or pray
- Engage in a hobby you enjoy

◆

MENTAL NEEDS

1. Make Your Mental Health a Priority

You are undergoing a stressful, uncertain time. How are you faring, psychologically?

If you feel fine, great! Keep doing whatever you're doing.

If you need help handling your emotions, turn to Chapter 3. If you need help managing your thoughts, turn to Chapter 4.

If you need more help, find it. Reach out to trusted friends, support groups, or professionals.

If you are experiencing profound anger, anxiety, or depression—if you are contemplating harming yourself or others—or if you are having panic attacks (uncontrolled bursts of fear so intense they feel like heart attacks)—please seek professional help immediately. If you're unsure where to turn, ask your doctor.

2. Give Your Brain Regular Breaks

One alarming thing about undergoing a crisis is that our brains seem to be in overdrive and yet working more slowly. We may have trouble putting our thoughts together or generating solutions for a problem. We might have difficulty retrieving the correct word or name or phrase. Sometimes we can't find things we just had in our hands.

We can counteract this by taking regular mental breaks. If you are feeling overwhelmed or overloaded, pause. Take a few slow, deep breaths. Switch focus from whatever you were doing to something calming and pleasant. Pet your dog. Look at a photo of someone you love. Text a friend.

You can reduce stress by taking five-minute mini-breaks every hour (more on that on p. 88). You can cultivate calm with two- or three-minute mini-meditations throughout the day (p. 59).

Resist the urge to "power through" difficult times. You don't have to be so hard on yourself. To better cope with your crisis, be kind and gentle with yourself. Give your brain the breaks it needs.

3. Occupy Your Mind

Another option when you are feeling overwhelmed by your situation is to give your mind other things to do. Distract yourself by shifting your attention to more pleasant topics. What would you rather think about? What would you rather pay attention to?

When Patrice lost her job, she found herself in a constant state of fear and worry. It was exhausting and unhelpful. She found that the only way she could fully divert her brain from fretting about the future was to read novels. She could escape to someone else's life for a bit. The time she spent reading gave her relief from brooding about her situation.

When Dan's wife died unexpectedly, he found it difficult to concentrate on the hefty history and political books he usually preferred. He found himself reading the same paragraph over and over, without absorbing anything. He switched to lighter reading fare—magazines and short stories—as a way of keeping his mind busy.

What activities do you find engaging? What hobbies or leisure pursuits do you enjoy? What have you liked doing in the past? Are you interested in rekindling any former pastimes?

What about arts and crafts? If you are so inclined, these activities can be very therapeutic. It's easy enough to doodle or mess around with yarn or paint—and you are apt to find your mind happily diverted, oblivious to your current concerns for a while.

Are there absorbing activities you can share with others in your household? Board games or TikTok dance challenges or party games like charades?

How would you like to occupy your mind these days?

4. Nourish Your Mind

To the extent you feel up to it, you can use this interlude to feed or stretch your mind.

When Louisa was dealing with cancer, she spent part of her time rekindling her love of crossword puzzles. Maybe you'd like to catch up on your reading or listening to music or indulging in word games.

If you sing or play a musical instrument, you have a unique opportunity to flex your brain by practicing your repertoire or adding new pieces to it.

Is there something you'd like to learn? Is there a particular topic or subject you'd like to study? If you are interested in learning new skills or crafts or how to do something, it's easy to find free online lectures, lessons, tutorials, and instructions. Or maybe there is something your friends can teach you.

What about you? How can you make your favorite mental activities a part of your life as you deal with your crisis?

5. Acquire the Information You Need—Prudently

Regardless of the nature of your crisis, you are likely to require information as you seek options and solutions.

Finding reliable information is more complicated than it once was. Be picky about which sources you trust. To the extent possible, avoid hearsay, gossip, and random posts on social media. Aunt Mabel might swear by her ginger concoction as cure-all but better to trust the professionals when researching medical treatments. Rely on trusted sources, and verify information before believing it.

Another potential trap is over-researching things. It's natural to have an unquenchable thirst for information in times of uncertainty. It can also be a problem if find yourself engaging in endless research without action.

If you are prone to be a news junkie, in times of crisis you may find yourself obsessed, doom-scrolling for hours and hours. If that sounds like you, find ways to limit your exposure. Make it more difficult or less comfortable for you to indulge your news habit. If you tend to get your news online, limit your internet time.

◆

SPIRITUAL NEEDS

1. Nourish Your Spirit

By "spirit", I mean that part of you, deep down that is your core inner being. It's your consciousness. It's the unknown forces within that inspire and guide you. It's your soul.

A time of crisis is the perfect time to feed and fuel your inner being with your favorite spiritual practices. This might include:

- Praying
- Meditating
- Spending time in nature

- Expressing daily gratitude
- Reading inspirational texts
- Listening to inspirational songs or speakers
- Participating in groups or organizations that you find spiritually fulfilling

Which spiritual practices are already in your life? Which help you cope when you feel overwhelmed or angry or frightened?

In addition to your current spiritual practices, consider things you've done in the past that you found soothing as well as new ideas you haven't yet tried but would like to learn more about.

2. Seek Solace and Strength in Your Spiritual Beliefs

You have no control over what is unfolding. There is no way of anticipating all the fallout and consequences. If you believe that there are larger forces at work, that you are a part of something bigger, it can be easier to cope with whatever is going on.

Journal about your spiritual beliefs. Write down what you know to be true. What can you hold onto during this stressful, uncertain time?

What worries can you release to a higher power?

As you process what's going on, capture key thoughts to keep in mind. Remind yourself of your preferred beliefs every day. Here are some examples that my coaching clients have found helpful during challenging or uncertain times:

- *Knowing that I can't see the Big Picture, I trust the Universe.*
- *I let go. I release all fears and burdens for Spirit to manage and I am free to be at peace and loving.*
- *I dissolve any anxiety with Divine love and trust that all is well in my world.*

- *I stand aside and let Infinite Intelligence lift my burdens and fight my battles.*
- *The long arms of Spirit reach over people and conditions, managing this situation, protecting my interests, and devising perfect solutions.*
- *Spirit makes a way where there seems to be no way.*
- *I lovingly accept Divine protection and guidance from the Universe. I am safe.*
- *Divine activity is now operating in my mind, body, and affairs, whether I see it or not.*

◆

SOCIAL NEEDS

We are a fundamentally social species. We feel better when we connect with people we care about. We suffer when we feel socially isolated.

1. Suspend Judgment of Others

Under times of stress, people are sometimes not "their best." Just as you were encouraged to avoid judging yourself (p. 9), cut other people some slack. If someone is being a jerk, let it go. Avoid inferring their intentions. Just as you are undergoing a crisis, they might be too. Maybe they are going through a divorce or fighting cancer or grieving the loss of a loved one. Assume that people are doing the best they can, under the circumstances.

If someone in your family is behaving badly, understand that the stress your situation is affecting them too. If you kid is being a brat, for example, how can you temper your response?

Turn the other cheek. Treat people as you would like to be treated. People make mistakes. Let it go. Forgive and forget.

You have more pressing priorities than holding grudges and resentments (more on this in Chapter 6).

Be magnanimous to people holding views that differ from yours. Understand that they are probably not getting the same information that you are. They may be receiving news from sources that are filtering and framing events in alternative ways. Any given person or organization has their own agenda. They may promote certain narratives for their own reasons or benefit.

When you encounter different opinions, suspend judgment. To the extent possible, separate your thoughts about the person from your thoughts about their opinions. We are all humans, doing the best we can with the information and knowledge available to us.

2. Connect with People

During times of crisis there is a significant human need to reach out, to reconnect, and to share the experience. This is especially important for people living alone.

Connect with people you care about however you can—on the phone, via Facetime or Skype or Zoom or whatever else makes sense. Take advantage of the available technology to create special moments together. Have fun together. Share experiences. Express affection. Draw closer.

Have you lost touch with people in your past with whom you'd like to reconnect? Find them through common contacts or social media.

Reach out. Tell them you were thinking about them. Catch up. Exchange stories about your experiences. Reconnect.

3. Find Support

It's one thing to socialize. But sometimes, especially during a time of crisis, you may need more help.

Put together your own personal support system of trusted people. To whom can you turn for solace? To whom can you turn for advice?

What support do you have? To which groups, individuals, or resources can you turn for solace, guidance, or solutions?

If you are feeling lonely, reach out. Avoid the tendency to wait for others to contact you. That puts you in a "victim role" which can feel awful and lead to depression and worse.

Instead, take action. Pick up your phone. Call someone. Do you need more help? What groups or organizations can support you during this uncertain time? If you're not sure, ask people you trust. If you can, research online. There are ample associations offering virtual assistance.

If you need help, ask for it.

4. Help Others

Sometimes the most effective way to manage your own stress is by helping others. How might you assist others in this time of crisis?

What can you give? How can you contribute? How can you do good during your crisis?

This is especially important if you are someone who tends to get caught up in yourself. If your focus and concerns are mostly directed inwards—if you are fretting about your personal challenges and how things are unfolding for you—you can alleviate a great deal of stress by turning some energy outwards.

Begin with the basics: what can you give that is easy and free? How can you give others respect? What acts of kindness could you offer?

How can you share affection with people you care about?

Consider each of your household members (including pets).

What are their specific needs? How might you help them?

Make a list of other important people in your life. Include family, friends, neighbors, co-workers, and whomever else you care about. Is there someone in need of help you could provide?

What about your community? Are you able to volunteer in some way? How could you help? What skills or knowledge do you have that you could offer? What services could you provide? Can you pack lunches or do some community outreach via phone?

Do you have items you could donate? Do you have extra food or linens or cleaning supplies that someone else could put to good use?

If you'd like to donate financially, ensure you are giving to well-run, fiscally responsible organizations that do what they purport to do.

ACTIVITY

1. Make a list of people you could help. Be specific. Consider:
    - Friends
    - Family
    - Co-workers
    - Neighbors
    - Groups and organizations you belong to
    - Your community
    - The world
2. Beside each name or entity on your list, jot down a few ideas.
    - What might they need?
    - How could you help?
    - What could you give?
    - How could you contribute?
3. Review your lists and circle a few of your favorite ideas. Make them happen.

It feels good to help others. It will lift your spirits. It will help you better manage your current challenges.

One caveat, though: be prudent. If you feel that others are taking advantage of you—if you are over-giving or if you feel like a martyr—stop and make some adjustments. A helpful resource for doing so is Harriet Braiker's *The Disease to Please: Curing the People-Pleasing Syndrome.*

REALITY CHECK: YOUR FUNDAMENTAL NEEDS

The preceding sections have included many ways you can address your fundamental human needs during a time of crisis. It is unlikely you will want to do every one of them. Choose your favorites. Which seem appealing?

Start small. Give thought to baby steps you can take to ensure different areas of your life are getting attention. To the extent possible, give regular daily consideration to your fundamental needs—body, mind, spirit, and social.

HELPFUL DAILY PRACTICE
Consider Your Fundamental Needs

Every morning, answer the following questions:

- What's one thing I could do for my body today?
- What's one thing I could do for my mind today?
- What's one thing I could do for my spirit today?
- What's one social thing I could do today?

The idea here is to give yourself a daily reminder to attend to the basics. What are the simplest, easiest things you can do today for your body, mind, spirit, and social life? What will feel good?

What fits nicely into the rest of your plans for the day?

Sometimes one activity addresses more than one area. For example, today I'm Zooming with friends for a kimchi lesson. That will be social as well as a treat for my brain to learn something new.

To address the other areas, I plan to meditate (for my spirit) and do some yard work (as physical activity). I've chosen easy, pleasant activities that will feel good when I do them. It's easy to fit them into today's writing schedule. Meditation takes just two or three minutes, a couple of times a day. I can adjust how much yard work I do, depending on how my day unfolds.

When I do something for all four basic areas, my day and my life feel more balanced. I feel a little more human, no matter what pressing challenges I face.

If, however, the day slips by and I don't get around to, say, doing the yard work, I won't beat myself up. I'll be happy that I did attend to the other three basic areas.

Then I've got a choice: I can either substitute a different physical activity to sneak in some body work before bed—say five minutes of stretching—or I can cut myself some slack and let it go and make a point of giving my body more attention tomorrow. I can tackle the yard work or do a virtual yoga class or walk my dogs.

Now if a few days or a week go by and I'm consistently avoiding physical activity, then I'll make a point to explore the source of that resistance *(Why am I neglecting my body?)* and to address it *(What's the simplest, easiest thing I can do for my body right now?)*

As your time of crisis unfolds, you are stepping forward into an uncertain future. To the extent you are attending to your basic human needs, you will be better able to weather whatever unfolds.

Be aware of your physical, mental, spiritual, and social needs. Give gentle attention to the fundamentals. If you sense something is being neglected, make some adjustments. Take small steps to aim for balance.

If you find balance elusive, it might be that your emotions are running rampant. If that sounds like you, turn to Chapter 3 for ways to manage emotions during times of crisis.

CHAPTER 3

Handle Your Emotions

It is natural to feel strong emotions during a time of crisis. There may be valid things to mourn or grieve. There might be legitimate things to be angry about. *The situation isn't fair!* There may be justifiable things to fear. *Will there be physical pain? How will this all unfold? What will the future look like?*

You are likely to experience waves of different emotions at different times. Certain feelings—and periods of numbness—will ebb and flow as events unfold.

To the extent you are aware of what you are feeling—to the degree you can identify your emotions—you can take steps to handle them.

◆

EXAMINE YOUR FEELINGS

What are you feeling right now? How is your mood? What emotions can you detect? How are they manifesting in your body and behavior?

ACTIVITY

1. Take a moment to focus on your emotions. *For best results, actually jot down your answers.* What are you feeling right now? To what extent do you detect anger, fear, stress, or any other emotions? To what extent are you numb?
2. Scan your body. Where do you detect tension or discomfort?
3. If you are uncertain about what you are feeling, are there clues in your recent behavior? For example, have you been snapping at loved ones, or crying, or overreacting to little annoyances? Has your sleep been affected? Have you been missing meals or overeating or overindulging in your preferred vices?

Are you experiencing any strong emotions like fear, anger, or grief?

If not, you may wish to skip ahead to a different chapter. Return here when you wish.

If, however, you are grappling with strong emotions, please continue reading. Begin by dispelling the internal charge inherent in what you are feeling.

◆

DISPEL STRONG EMOTIONS

Strong emotions are a natural and important part of the human experience. We are born with "fight or flight" responses ingrained in our DNA. Our bodies respond instantly to potential harm by either ramping up for battle or causing us to run away.

This involuntary reaction is meant to protect us—and it does. We get angry when provoked. Our bodies startle when we see sudden movements aimed towards us. We lash out or bolt from danger, fueled by adrenaline and a brief cascade of biochemical responses.

Under normal circumstances, this reaction is healthy and brief. It helps us deal with an emergency, then dissipates quickly.

In modern society, however, the "fight or flight" response can get hijacked or thrown into overdrive. When we experience frequent, chronic, or extreme stressors, our hearts keep pumping, our bodies churn out biochemicals like crazy, our guts keep twisting, and our negative emotions run rampant. The longer we stay in this state of chronic stress, the more damage we do to our bodies. We suffer heart problems, hypertension, and many other unhealthy consequences of unchecked stress.

In times of crisis, our "fight or flight" responses are running wild. We're in danger! We have no control over the situation! The future is uncertain!

So how to manage this vivid, involuntary, physical reaction? Begin by acknowledging your feelings. They are valid. They are your body's natural way of registering danger.

Next, be aware that it is unhelpful and unhealthy to remain in this heightened sense of emotion. You need to curtail and manage your feelings to better cope with the situation.

It is possible to interrupt the "fight or flight" cascade by, for example, slowing your breath. When you take deep, slow, deliberate breaths, you give your body the opportunity to recover from the biochemical assault.

To the extent possible, remove yourself from triggers or sources of strong emotion.

Distract yourself with other tasks for a few minutes. Do something—anything—to put your attention on something else. Clean something. Make a cup of tea. Read a few pages of a book.

You can use your clever brain to help, too. Reach for any thought that feels better. Replace *"I'm going to lose my job"* with something like, *"I might lose my job and if I do, I will find other work."* The former sentiment is a statement of certain doom. The latter thought offers the notion that there may be safe ways forward. Which feels better?

The point is to disrupt the negative emotional energy however you can.

TECHNIQUE
Dispel Strong Negative Emotions

When you detect that you are experiencing strong negative emotions:

1. Pause. Take three deep, slow, conscious breaths. As you do, count to five as you breathe air fully into your lungs. Count to five as you gently release the air you are holding.
2. Disrupt what you're feeling:
    - To the extent possible, remove yourself from the source of your negativity—even temporarily.
    - Distract yourself with something neutral or positive.
    - Reach for a thought that feels better.
3. Identify the thought behind the negative emotion.
4. Write down other ways to view the situation.
   Keep writing until you find a thought that feels better.

If you find that you are experiencing frequent or chronic negative emotions, try the following technique.

TECHNIQUE
Relax and Release

Clear a few minutes. Close your eyes and scan your body for any tension. When you detect an area under stress, place your hand on it. Breathe slowly and deeply. Physically relax. Imagine that you are releasing this tension out of your body. Keep focusing on relaxing this area of your body until you detect some relief.

Continue scanning your body. When you find another area of tension, place you hand there. Breathe slowly and deeply. Relax and release.

During stressful periods, you can use this method as an ongoing practice, once or more a day.

Once you have dispelled the initial "fight or flight" reaction, you will be better able to process your emotions and deal with them.

This chapter offers a variety of ways to manage the most common responses times of crisis, specifically:

- Sadness and grief (p. 39)
- Anger (p. 42)
- Fear and anxiety (p. 45)

It concludes with techniques to reduce stress and cultivate calm as you undergo whatever is unfolding in your life (p. 55).

Please turn to the section(s) that are most relevant for you right now. See which techniques are most effective for you.

Important note: if you are experiencing profound anger, anxiety, or depression—for example, if you are contemplating harming yourself or others—or if you are having panic attacks (uncontrolled bursts of fear so intense they feel like heart attacks)—please seek professional help immediately. If you're unsure where to turn, ask your doctor.

◆

MANAGING SADNESS AND GRIEF

Take a moment to identify the things about the current situation that make you sad.

> ACTIVITY
>
> Take a few minutes to journal, using the following prompts. Complete the sentences as many times as you wish.
>
> - *I'm sad that...*
> - *It breaks my heart that...*
> - *I feel hurt...*

It's natural and healthy to express sadness. You've felt sorrow before in your life. How did you process it? What helped? What didn't?

What can you apply now, to help you handle your current feelings?

> ACTIVITY
>
> 1. In general, when you feel sad:
>   - What do you do? How do you show your sadness?
>   - How do you cope? What works well for you?
>   - What doesn't?
> 2. What can you do now to work through your feelings of sadness? (Do it.)

In times of crisis, it's important to acknowledge, validate and grieve your losses. You may be mourning things like:

- Loss of safety
- Loss of security
- Loss of health
- Loss of life

- Loss of loved ones
- Loss of social contact
- Loss of your daily routine
- Loss of control over your schedule
- Loss of freedom
- Loss of things you had planned
- Loss of choice
- Loss of employment
- Loss of identity
- Financial loss
- Loss of opportunities
- Loss of culture
- Loss of time

Unfortunately, in any crisis, some of these losses are inevitable, unavoidable, unchangeable, and uncontrollable. There is little you can do to alter what's happening.

To cope, you need to accept the things you cannot change.

If you don't accept the situation, you are resisting reality. Resistance is futile. It doesn't change a thing. It feels awful. It keeps you stuck in a "victim" mentality. *"This horrible thing is happening to me and I can't do anything about it!"*

Yes, this horrible thing is happening and it is not being done "to" you. It is occurring regardless of you. It just "is". It happens to be affecting you.

Acceptance doesn't mean you approve of what's happening. It doesn't mean you are supposed to feel good about it. It means that you acknowledge that this is happening and that you have to deal with it.

Accept that you are undergoing a crisis. Accept that there will be inevitable losses. How can you cope with the situation? What support do you have available? Who can help you?

How can you make the best of the situation? For example, are there any steps you can take to address any of your losses? Action will help you heal. Doing something to improve your situation will make you feel better. Helping others (pp. 29–30) is a particularly effective way to mitigate grief.

ACTIVITY

Journal about the following:

- What losses are affecting you?
- How are you responding?
- What is helping you cope?
- What isn't? What adjustments are needed?
- What support and help do you have available?
- How can you foster acceptance under the circumstances?
- How can you make the best of the situation?
- What steps can you take to address any of your losses?
- Who can you help?

It is unreasonable to expect yourself to be able to flip a mental switch to turn off your sadness. Aim for progress. Focus on feeling better gradually.

To the extent possible, look for glimmers of good in your day. Even in the midst of your crisis, there are moments of happiness, peace, and kindness. Seek them and savor them. Make note of them.

If you are having difficulty coping with sadness and grief, please reach for help. There are numerous online and community resources available. If you don't know where to turn, ask your doctor.

♦

MANAGING ANGER

During any crisis or stressful situation, you may be harboring anger without realizing it.

ACTIVITY

Clear some time for thoughtful reflection and journaling. Be candid.

1. When you are angry, what does it feel like? Where in your body do you detect it?
2. How do you tend to express your anger? What actions do you take?
3. Describe a time when you did not handle your anger or frustration well. Describe what happened? What did you do? What were the consequences?'
4. Describe a time when you did manage your anger or frustration well. Describe what happened? What did you do? What were the consequences?
5. Given your answers, how would you like to process your current or future anger? What else would you like to try?

Next, shift focus to your present circumstances.

ACTIVITY

1. To what extent are you aware of being angry today?
2. What does your anger feel like? Where in your body do you detect it?
3. How have you been expressing your anger? How has your anger shown in your recent behavior?
4. As fast as you can, complete the following sentence fragments. Begin with the first one and complete it as many times as you can before moving onto the next.

- *I don't like...*
- *I feel frustrated..*
- *I am angry that...*

- *I am annoyed...*
- *It's not fair that...*
- *I want...*

Your anger may be valid, but it isn't helpful in its raw, unbridled state. Anger doesn't change anything. It is likely to be causing pain for you and the people around you. To the extent that you can process your anger and move on, you will be sparing your body, brain, and loved ones distress.

First, ask if this thing you are angry about is changeable. If so, do something to improve the situation. Every challenge has multiple possible solutions. What actions can you take in this instance?

If it isn't changeable—if you have no control over what is unfolding—if there is nothing you can do to affect the situation—your only effective option is to change your response to what's happening.

Can you modify your thoughts about what's happening? Can you alter what you're doing? Can you release your anger in a safe, healthy way? Can you turn it into something productive? For example, if you are frustrated at the lack of treatments available to cure a loved one, can you channel your energy into making them comfortable? Can you organize a fundraising campaign for relevant research?

Inherent in an angry thought is the assumption that something is "bad". To the extent you can suspend or defer that judgment, you will give yourself space to think about it differently.

Remind yourself that this person, place, thing, or situation just "is". It may not be to your liking. It may seem "bad" at the moment but you may be looking at it through a dark and very narrow lens.

Consider the possibility that your first impression is incorrect. A challenging experience can have silver linings. Something that appears to be a massive setback might, in fact, end up yielding unforeseen benefits. What seems like a terrific opportunity at first blush might end up, in the long term, being the worst experience in your life.

For example, let's say you lose your job. That seems "bad", right? Now imagine that by being unemployed, you get to stay home and relax for the first time in a long while. That would make your unemployment "good", right? But maybe as time goes by your unemployment makes you angry, anxious, and depressed, which seems "bad". Except you are motivated you to go out and find different work, which you actually like better than your previous job. That would seem to be "good". But what if your best friend is jealous of your new position, or your work gets sabotaged by a new co-worker or...you get the idea.

All can you know for sure is that this situation just "is"—especially during crises or uncertain times. To the extent you can suspend labeling the situation, you can reduce its inherent emotional charge. Endeavor to short-circuit your anger by taking action...to do what makes sense to proceed.

It's helpful to rewrite an angry thought to be more accurate. For example, *"Losing my job will be a disaster"* could be re-written as *"Losing my job might be a disaster...or it might be a blessing in disguise... or it might be the best thing that's ever happened to me... or it might have relatively little impact in the long run. The truth is I really don't know how this will turn out so there's no point jumping to conclusions. I must wait and see how things unfold."*

TECHNIQUE
Process an Angry Thought

1. Review your answers to Question 4 mentioned in the previous activity. Choose one item.
2. With that item in mind, journal about the following:
   - What labels have you attached to this item? How could you rewrite it to be more accurate?
   - To what extent is this item changeable?
   - What extent is this out of your control?
   - To what extent is acceptance required here?
   - What actions can you take to improve the situation?
   - How might you think differently about the situation? What thoughts might feel better? *For example, "This situation is temporary."*
   - What can you do to release your anger about this in a safe, healthy, responsible way? (Consider your answers to the questions on p. 42).
3. Take steps to address the item you circled. If there are actions you can take, do so.

Bonus Activity: repeat this technique for any other item(s) you would like to process.

◆

REDUCE YOUR FEARS

There is much to fear during a crisis. A jumble of frightening feelings can build into a chronic cloud of debilitating anxiety. To reduce your fears, it's helpful to tease them apart and deal with them, one by one. What, in particular, is causing you fear?

ACTIVITY

Clear some uninterrupted time. As fast as you can, complete the following sentence fragments. Begin with the first one and complete it as many times as you can before moving onto the next.

I'm nervous that...
I worry about...
I'm afraid that...
I'm anxious about...
I'm concerned that...
I'm fearful that...
I'm frightened that...
I'm terrified of...

As soon as you begin to articulate your fears, congratulate yourself for being brave enough to so do. Be kind and gentle with yourself.

Know that whatever discomfort arises, it is temporary. As soon as you identify your true concerns, you can address them.

Select one fear you've identified. Choose an item that seems especially vivid today. With this fear in mind, work through the process that follows:

1. Examine Your Fear

How, and under what circumstances, is your fear affecting your current life? How does it affect you? How does it affect the people around you?

Consider that this fear is present for good reason. It may be protecting you. It may be benefiting you or serving you in various ways. Or maybe a similar fear did so in the past.

Alas, despite any benefits it may confer, your fear also has costs. It may take a physical or mental toll. It may prevent you from taking advantage of certain opportunities. It might create stress, sleep problems, eating disorders, or substance abuse. It could be affecting the people close to you.

Next, it's helpful to remind yourself of the benefits you might get by overcoming this fear. How would you feel to be free of this fear? What would you rather be feeling? What would you rather be thinking or doing?

Take a moment to pretend how you would feel if you could let go of your fears, doubts, and anxiety. Imagine your relief! You would feel so much better. It would be easier on your brain and body. You would be able to operate more effectively during these stressful uncertain times. You would be more pleasant to be around. You would be better able to help others.

Have you dealt with fear in the past? What helped you reduce your anxiety? What didn't? What can you apply to help you cope with your current situation?

What support do you have available to help you deal with this fear? To what people or groups can you turn?

Next, challenge yourself to think about your fear differently. Temper it. Dispute it. Generate evidence to the contrary.

For example, if your fear is "*I'm afraid I'll get sick*" you might contest it with something like, "*I hope I don't get sick but if I do, I'll handle it. I will do what my doctor says to maximize my chances for a complete recovery.*"

Bonus points if you can find any humor in the situation. *Omigod, I sound like my hypochondriac aunt Betty!* Laughter offers an instant relief from stress and negativity.

Finally, it's important to ask yourself: What would you rather believe? For example, "*I am healthy. I am taking good care of myself and my family.*"

TECHNIQUE
Examine Your Fear

1. How is this fear affecting your life? When does it arise? How does it affect you? How does it manifest in your body, your thoughts, and your actions?
2. How is this fear affecting the people close to you?
3. How is this fear serving you? What protection is this fear giving you? What benefits are you presently getting from this fear?
4. What is this fear costing you?
5. What would be the benefits of overcoming this fear? How would it feel to be free of this fear? What would you rather be feeling? What would you rather be thinking or doing?
6. Have you experienced this fear in the past? How did you address it? What worked well for you? What didn't? What can you apply to the current situation?
7. What support do you have available? To what or whom can you turn?
8. How could you re-frame this fear? Is this fear valid? Is it really true? What evidence is there to the contrary? What is the real truth here? What is the objective reality? Write out as many refutations as you can.
9. Is there any humor in this? Is there something you might look back and laugh about in the distant future?
10. What would you rather believe? Be specific and detailed.

I strongly encourage you to work through one fear right now.

When you feel called to do so, use the technique to work through another fear. Pace yourself gently so that you work through your fears in a way that is comfortable for you.

2. Understand That Whatever Happens, You'll Handle It

Susan Jeffers has made a career out of helping people overcome fears by taking action. She makes the point that EVERYONE is afraid, so it's no biggie that you are. Your fear will grow until you take action.

So..."feel the fear and do it anyway".

Dr Jeffers's recommended mantra to overcome fear is to remind yourself that "whatever happens, I'll handle it." She advocates countering fear-inducing "what if's" with "I'll handle it." For example:

What if I get sick? I'll handle it!

What if I lose my job? I'll handle it.

What if an earthquake/hurricane/tornado hits? I'll handle it.

It may sound simplistic, so let me bolster it a bit. Consider that you have handled everything in your life thus far. You have solved problems and overcome challenges.

ACTIVITY

1. As fast as you can, write down ten challenging situations you handled.
2. Journal a bit. Convince yourself that if you could get through those situations, you can get through your crisis.

Bear in mind that you have the capacity to handle much worse situations than you have already encountered. Human beings can handle dire, demanding situations. People survive trauma, abuse, addiction, injuries, and devastating illnesses.

It's also helpful to contemplate possible solutions for the thing you fear. For example, one of my coaching clients is a successful entrepreneur who was grappling with a profound, persistent fear that a particular horrible scenario would unfold. He was distraught.

"What if X happens? I'll lose my business!"

"Okay, so let's say X occurs and you lose your business," I said. "What would you do if that happened?"

"Why I'd start another business," he said, matter-of-factly, and then he instantly laughed out loud. "You're right! It's not the end of the world. I'd just start another business." He knew, without question, his fear was groundless. He enjoyed every aspect of the entrepreneurial process. Should something cause him to lose his business, he'd simply launch a new one.

Nancy was anxious about her elderly mother, who was stuck alone in a nursing care facility during the pandemic. "She's frail. She's depressed. She's at risk to get infected."

"That's challenging. How are you handling it?"

"My sister and I are calling her every day using FaceTime so she can see us. We are reminding her how to stay safe and why it's important for her to stay sequestered. Our kids are phoning her too, which she loves. I check in with the facility staff to see how she's doing and what she needs. We're sending care packages. For Mother's Day we went outside her window with signs saying we love her."

Try it now. What are the "what if's" that are most distressing for you? For each, think about it. Should this thing happen, it might be unpleasant, it might be challenging...but you *would* get through it. You've dealt with everything you've experienced so far in your life...and you will handle whatever else comes up.

Next, give yourself the opportunity to imagine some possible solutions, should this horrible thing arise. For example, should you lose your job, you would research options and do what makes sense. You would search for new work. You would mine the situation for new opportunities. You would apply for the grants or funds for which you qualify. You would put in place the support you need. You would find a way of coping with the experience. You are a competent, resourceful, clever person. You would get through it.

ACTIVITY

1. List the "what if's" that are most distressing for you.
2. Read your list out loud. As you do, add "I'll handle it!"
   What if ____________? Answer: I'll handle it!
3. Take one item from your list and brainstorm possible solutions. Should this horrible thing arise, how would you handle it? What actions would you take to get through the experience? What support might you have?

3. Recognize the Futility of Worry.

Anxiety is a visceral reaction to uncertainty. Our hands shake. Our pulse races. We become short of breath. It can feel like there is an iron band tightening around our chests. Our thinking gets muddled and panicky. Worry feels awful. It makes the situation more difficult and stressful for ourselves—and it's unpleasant for our loved ones.

Fretting about what might happen does not actually influence future outcomes. Sorry to say it but you are not that powerful. Whatever is happening in the world will unfold regardless of how much you worry.

ACTIVITY

1. Think about a time when you worried about something in the hopes of improving the outcome. Describe what happened.
2. Ask your logical self the following questions:

   - What was the actual impact of your worry?
   - How did it affect you?
   - How did it affect others?
   - To what extent did your worrying affect the outcome?

Your worry doesn't work. Convince yourself of its futility.

ACTIVITY

Write out the following sentences five times, slowly and deliberately:

My worry is not changing how things are unfolding.

My worry will not improve the outcomes.

As you write, add compelling thoughts, reasons, and rationales to remind or convince you of the truth of these statements.

Given that your anxiety isn't helping you or anyone else, it's important to find ways to reduce it.

4. Take Action

Okay, so simply worrying doesn't help. However, if there *is* something you could be doing that will improve the situation, by all means do it. *I can't cure my cancer but I can eat nourishing food. I can rest my body as much as possible. I can pray and meditate. I can chat with my most positive friends. I can volunteer to read to children at the library.*

Taking action—any action—even a tiny step—feels much better than sitting there worrying. Action, unlike worry, *could* affect how things unfold.

ACTIVITY

1. What actions can you take that will improve your current situation?
2. Make a list.
3. Circle one action you would like to try.
4. Do it right now. (Or as soon as is feasible.)

If you get stuck, turn to Chapter 5 for ways forward.

5. Distract Yourself

How can you interrupt your anxiety with distractions? What can you do to otherwise engage yourself in a healthy way?

Can you busy yourself with work or domestic tasks?

Does interacting with friends or family reduce your level of fear? Can you get lost in a book, a puzzle, or a creative project?

ACTIVITY

What are healthy ways you can distract yourself? Make a list. (More on healthy distractions on p. 78.)

6. Body Scan

The following technique is scientifically proven to reduce anxiety, chronic pain, and depression. Take a few minutes to try it now.

TECHNIQUE
Body Scan

Lie down and close your eyes. Scan each part of your body, putting your attention on one area at a time. As you focus on a given spot, notice the level of tension in that area, then release any you detect.

Take turns focusing on and relaxing your left foot, left ankle, left shin, left knee, left thigh, right foot, left hip, right ankle, right shin, right knee, right thigh, right hip, groin, lower abdomen, upper abdomen, chest, neck, face, jaw, left shoulder, left upper arm, left forearm, left wrist, left palm, left fingers, right shoulder, right upper arm, right forearm, right wrist, right palm, right fingers.

This can be done to calm oneself whenever anxiety flares up. It's also highly beneficial as a regular, daily practice.

7. Consider EFT Tapping

Although the research is inconclusive, some people find that a technique called Emotional Freedom Technique (EFT) Tapping reduces their anxiety. It involves focusing on one issue or concern while tapping with one hand on a prescribed series of locations on your body.

It's most easily learned by following along with a demonstration, so if you'd like to try it, do an online search for a video of "EFT tapping anxiety". See if it gives you some relief.

8. Fake it 'Til You Make It

If all else fails, you may have to pretend. Hide your fears and anxiety from others and from yourself. Act as if you are supremely confident. The more you can play the role of a calm, unruffled being, the less fear you'll actually experience.

This may sound like a cop-out but very successful people use this technique. Oscar-winning actors report that despite their success, they still experience stage fright—and that to get through it they must pretend all is well until their nerves settle. Grammy-winners including Beyoncé and Lady Gaga have created fierce alter egos to give them the courage to perform.

Look around for role models. Who can you emulate? If you can pretend to be calm and confident—if you can act that way even for a little bit—you will give your brain and body a respite from the biochemical burden of the fear response. The more you can act composed, the longer the periods you reduce your anxiety, the closer you will be to reducing your fears.

Meanwhile, look for ways to cultivate calm in the midst of your crisis.

◆

REDUCE STRESS AND CULTIVATE CALM

To the extent you can foster tranquility within and around yourself, you will reduce your anxiety and temper its ill effects on yourself and others. What follows are seven ways to do so.

1. Reduce Unnecessary Stressors

You are going through a crisis. Some sources of your stress are unavoidable. However, take a moment to identify any stressors that you *could* reduce or eliminate. What are you subjecting yourself to that you really don't have to? What can you limit, delegate, or otherwise avoid? What can you pay someone else to do? What could you barter or trade?

ACTIVITY

1. List your current sources of stress.
2. For each, ask: how could this be reduced or eliminated?

2. Take Breaks

Take regular breaks in your day. Five-minute mini-breaks, hourly, can work wonders. Whatever you are doing, pause on the hour to do something else. Aim for healthy, peaceful breaks—doing things that soothe or revive you—rather than unhealthy, obsessive, or stress-inducing activities. Stretch, breathe, or fetch a cup of tea instead of cramming in a quick social media blitz.

ACTIVITY

1. What are healthy, helpful, peaceful five-minute breaks for you?
2. What would be unhealthy or unhelpful breaks for you?

Ideally, intersperse these mini-breaks throughout your day.

HELPFUL DAILY PRACTICE
Five-Minute Breaks Every Hour

Use a timer to ensure you give yourself five-minute breaks every hour. Choose from your list of healthy, helpful, and/or peaceful activities listed above.

Avoid the unhealthy or unhelpful activities you've identified.

3. Scrutinize Your Technology

How is your technology affecting you during your crisis? Which devices are helping you cope? Perhaps your phone is providing a lifeline by connecting you with others. Maybe you've found some great relaxation apps.

What is causing you stress? Is your phone pinging with too many stress-provoking notifications? Maybe your computer is a great source of information and activities...except that you can get sucked into social media or web surfing in an unhealthy, addictive way. Maybe you would be better to limit the amount of time you spend online.

What about you? What technology is helping you? What is not? What adjustments can you make to cultivate calm? What technology can you turn off or avoid? What do you need to limit?

ACTIVITY

1. What technology is helping you cope with your crisis?
2. What is not? What technology is causing your stress or anxiety? What feels unhealthy or unhelpful?
3. What can you do to limit or avoid any technology that causes you anxiety?

4. Unplug Altogether

Technology takes a toll on us. Our minds and bodies were not designed to interact with technology as much as we do these days.

Studies have proven that the more time we spend completely "unplugged", the greater the improvement in our physical and psychological well-being.

For the past decade or so, I have advocated the benefits of taking regular "Technology Vacations." I encourage my coaching clients to spend a few hours—or a day—or a weekend—unplugged. No phone, no television, no laptop, no internet, no electronic games.

Kevin found great relief to shut off his phone and laptop after dinner. He found it fulfilling and restorative to focus on his family.

Teresa balked at this at first. She didn't want to be unreachable. She didn't want to miss out on the latest news. However, once she tried turning off her tech for a few hours every weekend, she saw the value in it. She used the time to do things that felt better. She puttered in her garden. She napped. She resurrected a long-forgotten knitting project. She didn't miss any vital phone calls. She felt calmer and healthier. She found that she could easily catch up on her email, voice mail, and the news when she turned her technology back on. In fact, she now makes it a regular practice to spend each Saturday unplugged.

To the extent you can remove yourself from technology altogether, for whatever period of time you can during your crisis, you will reduce your anxiety.

HELPFUL WEEKLY PRACTICE
Unplug

Designate a technology-free period of time for yourself each week. For whatever period of time you choose—an afternoon, a day or more—turn off your computer, phone, electronic games, etc.

While you're unplugged, consider this next remedy.

5. Spend Time in Nature

Another proven stress-buster is to go outdoors. As mentioned in Chapter 2, our bodies crave fresh air and sunshine. Any time you can spend in nature works wonders in reducing anxiety and fostering health. How can you spend time outside?

If you live in a rural area, this is relatively easy. Just make a point of spending some time outside every day. Studies have shown that just five minutes outdoors is a mood-lifter.

If you don't live in a rural area, challenge yourself to find creative solutions. Can you walk around the neighborhood? Are there times of the day or evening when it's easier to do so? Do you have access to parks or pets or gardens or window boxes anywhere? Do you have access to a porch where you can sit in the sun for a while? Can you open a window to breathe in fresh air?

If you can't get outside, can you trick your body into thinking that you are? For example, can you order a light therapy lamp or swap some light bulbs for full spectrum versions that mimic sunlight?

6. Meditate

The psychological and physiological benefits of meditation are many and profound. Besides improving your focus, meditation is a proven stress reducer. Almost every bodily system functions better when you meditate regularly. Meditation has been proven to be an effective remedy for low mood, depression, and anxiety. For many, meditation is also a spiritual practice that brings solace, comfort, and meaning to its practitioners. The added value of meditation is that it gives your brain a temporary break from the swirl of emotions and thoughts about your concerns.

If you already have a meditation practice, wonderful! Please skip ahead to the next point.

If, however, you don't meditate, please read on. Despite all the potential benefits of meditation, what often stops people from giving it a whirl is the misconception that meditation requires grueling, boring and/or inconvenient long sessions. The truth is that you can derive all the psychological and physiological benefits of meditation through very brief sessions—just two or three minutes long—sprinkled through your day.

In fact, according to meditation guru Yongey Mingyur Rinpoche, it is better to aim for very short mini-meditation sessions than to tackle longer sessions.

How convenient! It's easy enough to take a two- or three-minute meditation break between tasks. It's not difficult. It's not complicated. It's just a matter of doing it. If you actually take a few brief meditation breaks every day, you will experience cognitive and health benefits. Please try the following activity right now:

TECHNIQUE
Mini-Mediation

Set a timer for three minutes.

Sit quietly, eyes closed. Clear your mind. Breathe. Just "be." Gently push aside any thoughts that come up and refocus your attention on your breathing. Aim to think of absolutely nothing. When your mind wanders (and it will), avoid berating yourself. Simply clear your mind again. There is no wrong way to do this. Keep going until the timer buzzes.

Two mini-medications a day can benefit every system in your body. The more you meditate, the greater the rewards. You are likely to feel happier and healthier and calmer. Try it this week and see.

7. Focus on "Now"

One fundamental way to cultivate calm is to shift focus from fretting about the future to living in the present moment.

Hopefully, you got a glimpse of that during the mini-meditation in the preceding section. When you are present in the here and now, there is nothing to be concerned about.

There's no reason to fuss or fret or worry. Right now, in this moment, all is well. Even in the middle of your crisis. The more you practice being present, the more you shift your attention to just "being", the more personal peace you will experience. Whatever you are doing, give it your full attention. Fully experience this moment.

Be present. Whatever you're doing, do it mindfully. If you're eating a meal, focus on the taste, scent, appearance, and texture of your food.

If you're working out, focus on your breathing and your form, rather than the fourteen things you need to do later. If your spouse needs you to find something, do what is less disruptive to you: either ask if it can wait until you are done your current task or locate it and then resume whatever you were doing before you were interrupted.

Avoid multi-tasking. Sure, you have many tasks to do...but if you focus on only one thing at a time, you'll reduce stress. If you're playing with your kids, focus on them and only them. If you're working on a project, focus on that and only that, to the extent possible. Do your best to compartmentalize activities and to minimize interruptions.

If this is new for you, give it a try. For the next few days, set a timer to go off at different times of the day. When it does, assess your focus.

What are you doing? To what extent are you fully engaged?

What are you doing? Are you multi-tasking or is your attention on only one thing?

What are you thinking about? Are you dwelling in the past, fretting about the future, or focused on the present?

HELPFUL DAILY PRACTICE
Shift Focus to Now

Set some alarms for random times during your day.

Whenever an alarm goes off, pause and check the focus of your attention.

If your attention is focused on one and only one thing, wonderful!

If you are multi-tasking, stop. Select one activity and give it your complete attention.

If you are thinking about the past, shift focus to what you can do here and now. You can't alter what's happened. What are your present options?

If you are worrying about the future, pause and ask: is there anything I can do now that could alter the outcome? If so, do so. If not, release it and allow events to unfold without worry or drama. Rest assured that whatever happens, you'll handle it.

Once you take the reins of your emotions, give attention to your thoughts. The next chapter focuses on how to manage the tornado of ideas that can arise in the times of crisis.

CHAPTER 4

Manage Your Mind

As you deal with your crisis, your busy brain is probably juggling a jumble of ideas, beliefs, and tasks. There are daily challenges to solve and a constant flurry of information to sort out. You may also be dealing with the burden of other people's ideas, concerns, and opinions. There is a lot to process.

What thoughts are occupying your mind as you go through your crisis? Are you repeating dire messages to yourself? Are you looking for the good in what's happening? Are you doubting yourself? Are you appreciating unforeseen benefits of your experiences? Are you berating yourself for something you should have done or not done?

Protect your mind during this time of crisis. Curate your thoughts. Identify the ideas you want to harbor—those that are helpful and healthy. Reject or transform the ideas that make you feel bad.

The thoughts and beliefs that are foremost in your mind play a major part in determining the nature of your current experience.

However, most people are unaware of their inner dialog and how it is affecting them—especially in the midst of stressful, uncertain circumstances.

Pause for a moment to take stock. What's going on in your mind right now?

ACTIVITY

1. Set a timer for five minutes. Writing (or typing) as quickly as you can, jot down whatever thoughts enter your head.
2. When the timer buzzes, review your responses.

   - Put a check mark beside any thought that seems helpful or healthy.
   - Circle any thought that seems unhelpful or unhealthy.

Once you start to tease apart what you are thinking, you can begin to manage what's happening in your mind. You can highlight positive, helpful, healthy thoughts and remind yourself of them daily. You can counter unhelpful, unhealthy beliefs and modify them into ideas that will better serve you. This chapter provides techniques to do just that.

◆

CULTIVATE HELPFUL THOUGHTS

Begin by collecting your preferred beliefs. To the extent you can cultivate positive thoughts you can steel yourself to weather your crisis.

1. Keep Track of Good Thoughts

Begin with the positive ideas of which you are already aware.

ACTIVITY

1. Create a running List of Good Thoughts somewhere handy—in your phone, on your computer, in your journal, on index cards—whatever will work for you.
2. Begin by copying all the helpful, healthy ideas and beliefs you checked off in the previous activity.

3. As you do so, capture any other positive thoughts that occur to you.
4. Going forward, review this list every morning and whenever else you'd like refresh your mind with helpful, healthy thoughts.
5. Add new positive, helpful, or healthy thoughts as they occur to you.

2. Look for the Good in the Situation

No matter how challenging the circumstances, good things happen. Michael J. Fox was diagnosed with Parkinson's at age thirty, derailing a wildly successful acting career. He fostered good by founding a research foundation, becoming an advocate for people with Parkinson's, and writing inspirational books about staying positive, no matter what. He found new personal strength and an enriched, deepened relationship with his wife Tracy Pollan.

Holocaust survivor Viktor Frankl noted the human kindnesses and simple pleasures he witnessed in the concentration camps. The beauty of a bird seemed so profound, he wept with joy to witness it. He turned down a chance to escape to stay behind and help people. In doing so, he found his own purpose in life and founded a school of psychotherapy (logotherapy) to help others do the same.

Children's television personality Mr. Rogers told this story about when he was a boy and would see scary things on the news: "My mother would say to me, 'Look for the helpers. You will always find people who are helping.' To this day, especially in times of disaster, I remember my mother's words, and I am always comforted by realizing that there are still so many helpers—so many caring people in this world."

What positive things do you see in the middle of your crisis? What good things have happened to you?

ACTIVITY

1. Journal about the positive things you've noticed during your crisis. Consider:
   - Acts of kindness
   - Silver linings
   - Benefits to your own life
   - Positive things in your community
   - New opportunities
2. Add your favorites to your List of Good Thoughts.

3. Savor Special Moments throughout Your Day

Life is precious. During trying times, little things can mean a lot. In the midst of a crisis, we can hold our loved ones a little closer. We can eat our meals mindfully, relishing eat bite. We can sing along to a favorite song on the radio. We can take pleasure in the scent of our favorite soap. We can drink in a sunset.

By focusing on life's little pleasures, we foster positive thoughts and feelings. Chrissy Dunn found daily gifts as she conquered stage III pancreatic cancer. "Every day is beautiful and I've learned to look at things as blessings that I used to just take for granted. The shoes I put on my feet, the hot water when I take a bath—every single aspect of my life is a blessing."

ACTIVITY

Today, make a point of savoring the simple pleasures you encounter.

Eat mindfully. Enjoy the sensation of water on your hands when you wash them. Seek pleasant scents, sounds, and textures. Pause to take in the view, wherever you are.

Imagine that you have a 3D camera in your head. Whenever you see something you want to capture, take a mental picture. Maybe you catch your kids or pets looking adorable *Click!* Perhaps you notice the lovely shape of the steam curling up from tea in your favorite mug. *Click!* Oh, look at the way the sun is lighting up that building *Click!*

ACTIVITY

Pretend that you have an internal 3D camera. As you go through your day, take mental pictures of the scenes and moments you want to remember.

4. Practice Daily Gratitude

It doesn't matter what's going on in our lives—there is always *something* to appreciate. We're breathing. We have water to drink. We have food and shelter. We have functioning brains.

Ample research has proven that if you look for ANYTHING about which you can feel thankful, you will start to feel better. It will also reduce stress, shift your focus to the present, elevate your mood, and improve your relationships.

In the midst of your crisis, gratitude can be plentiful and profound. When Sean was dealing with kidney disease, he thought:

I'm so thankful for the actions of the medical personnel because they are doing everything they can to help me.

I'm so grateful for the researchers developing treatments because they are working on new ways to heal myself and others.

I'm so thankful this experience has deepened my relationship with my wife because our marriage is so much stronger.

It's a powerful practice to express gratitude for what we have, who we are, and what we experience. It casts our lives in a more positive light. It shifts our focus to what's working well, rather than what's not.

Begin a daily practice of listing your blessings, no matter how small. (*I'm so grateful to sleep in my own bed because it's so much more comfortable than being in the hospital.)* Try beginning your morning by writing out five things for which you are grateful.

One caveat, though. Sometimes people try this practice and find that soon it deteriorates into a rote daily practice akin to writing out a shopping list. If you've tried this practice and found it lacking, do what Einstein did: rather than just listing the things for which you are grateful, write out the reason why.

This small alteration—the additional explanation of *why* we're grateful—elevates and deepens each item exponentially. Rather than jotting down "my friends" on a laundry list of gratitude bullet points, it's much more powerful to specify the reasons. For example: *"I'm so grateful for the phone calls from friends today because I feel loved and cared about."*

I call this practice Gratitude 2.0. I could list dozens of jaw dropping stories about the power of the practice of expressing daily gratitude...yet the best possible examples are from your own experience. Do yourself a favor: Try it for yourself. See what happens.

HELPFUL DAILY PRACTICE
Gratitude 2.0

Each morning, write down at least five things for which you're grateful— and specify why.

"I'm grateful for X because..."
"I'm so thankful for Y because..."
Aim for at least five different items every day.

There are two optional upgrades to this practice:

Optional Upgrade #1: Read your list out loud.

As you do, focus on really feeling gratitude for each item. You might sense a little relief or some positive energy that heightens your gratitude.

Optional Upgrade #2: Share your list with someone you trust.

Louisa found Gratitude 2.0 to be life-transforming. When she told her best friend Carole about it, they decided to join forces. They both make their gratitude lists every morning. Several times a week, they phone to read their most recent lists to each other.

"It takes five minutes and it makes the process so much more powerful," said Carole. Louisa added, "It's such an easy and lovely way to support each other. It seems to heighten our gratitude. Often, one of us will mention something that causes the other one to think of something else to add to our lists. It helps both of us appreciate our lives more."

5. Appreciate the People and Things You May Have Been Undervaluing

As you undergo your crisis, consider what you may have been taking for granted. It wasn't until a car accident sidelined her than Judy realized how important her basic mobility was. Residents of Flint, Michigan, took clean drinking water for granted until they didn't have it.

Also contemplate people you may have been taking for granted. Include people you know personally as well as strangers who provide you and others with goods and services. Crises reveal the true character of people around you as well as the genuine state of your relationships.

When her mother died unexpectedly, Lynn was overwhelmed with everything that needed to be done. Her relatives didn't lift a finger to help however Lynn's former high school friends did. She hadn't seen them in decades but they rolled up their sleeves and toiled for weeks to get things sorted at her mother's house. Through their kindness and generosity, Lynn learned who she could trust, who really cared about her, and which relationships she wanted to rekindle and foster.

ACTIVITY

1. What have you been taking for granted? Make a list.
2. Who have you been taking for granted? Consider people you know as well as strangers who provide you and others with goods and services.
3. Review your answers. Do these observations spark any positive perspectives on your crisis? If so, add them to your List of Good Thoughts.

6. Search for Different Perspectives and New Thoughts That Feel Better

Be proactive in curating your thoughts. Actively seek ideas that give you relief and comfort. Look for role models among the people around you. Who is looking on the bright side of things? Who is helping out?

Who is soothing you? To whom can you turn for advice or support? Who has a great attitude?

Be aware and appreciative of the positive and helpful people in your life. Gravitate to them. Thank them. Spend the time you can interacting with them. Learn from them. Emulate them.

ACTIVITY

1. Who are the positive people in your life? Make a list. Include the optimists, people who soothe you, those you turn to for advice and support.
2. What do they think about your crisis? How do they perceive it? What helpful perspectives do they have that you can add to your List of Good Thoughts?

As you go through your day, be on the look-out for other good thoughts. Maybe a stranger shares a helpful perspective that gives you a more positive outlook on what's happening to you. Perhaps you have a new insight that makes you feel better about what you are experiencing.

For example, you might remind yourself that there are multiple solutions for any problem. There are numerous ways to handle whatever comes up.

Consider that what you are experiencing is temporary. Yes, it is challenging, but this will not last forever.

Remember that you are in a much more fortunate position than many people on the planet at the moment. For example, think about places that are war-torn or that don't have clean or running water. Contemplate the extraordinary efforts required to keep things sanitary in those communities. How fortunate are we to have relatively easy ways to keep ourselves, our families, and our homes clean.

Remind yourself that you have the opportunity to learn and grow from whatever unfolds. Ask yourself: what am I learning as I go through this crisis? What are the lessons here? What are the opportunities?

Mull over some positive "What If's", such as:
What if a lot of good comes out of this?
What if great new opportunities arise for me and my family?

ACTIVITY

Be on the lookout for other thoughts, ideas, and perspectives that feel healthy and helpful.

Capture them in your List of Good Thoughts.

7. Carry Some Good Thoughts with You

Use your dominant hand as a reminder of some Good Thoughts. Try the following activity now.

TECHNIQUE
Four Good Thoughts

Look at your dominant hand.

Touch your thumb to your forefinger and remind yourself of a specific time you felt truly loved and cared about.

Touch your thumb to your middle finger. Recall a specific instance when you felt proud of yourself.

Touch your thumb to your ring finger. Remember a specific, significant way in which you've helped someone else.

Touch your thumb to your pinky finger. Remind yourself of a specific instance when you were truly happy.

Use this "handy" technique, when you feel stressed or unhappy. It's quick, unobtrusive, and guaranteed to lift your mood and shift your thoughts to happier, healthier topics.

While you are cultivating positive thoughts, it's equally important to detect and counter negative, unhelpful, or unhealthy thinking. It takes some effort. It takes practice. But it is possible to learn to temper negative thoughts. Even if you tend to be pessimistic, you have the capacity to deliberately transform your thinking patterns. To the extent you do, you will reduce stress and feel better, physically and mentally.

Begin by identifying and curtailing them at the source.

◆

REDUCE OR REMOVE SOURCES OF NEGATIVE THOUGHTS

Consider the mind sets of the people around you. Who is causing you undue stress? Who is spewing complaints, criticisms, and pronouncements of doom? Who is spouting fear and anxiety?

At the risk of stating the obvious: you have the right to protect yourself. If you are receiving a stream of negative or anxiety-provoking thoughts you owe it to yourself to reduce or remove their source.

We don't need Debbie Downers or Nervous Nellies in our lives when things are going well. It's even more important to suppress these voices when we are undergoing a crisis.

If particular people are stressing you out, bringing you down, or ramping up your anxiety, you would benefit from limiting your contact with them.

If you can't avoid them altogether, seek ways to reduce their influence on you. If your mom is a complainer, how can you deflect her concerns so they don't become rooted in your own thoughts? How can you side-step her negativity so it doesn't infect you? What can you do to shake off her worries and counter her pessimism?

ACTIVITY

1. Contemplate the people in your life.
   - Who is causing you stress?
   - Who being unnecessarily negative?
   - Who is causing you anxiety?
2. For each person you've named, answer the following:
   - What are they saying or doing that is unhelpful, unhealthy, or otherwise unpleasant for you?
   - What impact does this person have on you? How do you feel when you are with them?
   - How might you protect yourself? How could you reduce your contact with them?
   - If you can't avoid them altogether, how can you reduce their influence on you? How can you inoculate yourself from their concerns? How can you counteract their impact on your mood?
3. Take steps to limit contact from the people you have identified.
4. Going forward, be on the lookout. Shield yourself from people who are unnecessarily negative or fearful.

Apply the same approach to information you receive from the media. If certain publications, websites, social media platforms, or public personas are causing you distress, you would do well to avoid them or to limit your exposure to them.

COUNTER NEGATIVE THOUGHTS

Much as we can try to avoid or limit our exposure to negative thoughts, they still sprout up, especially during stressful, uncertain times. When they do, it's important to mitigate them. Process them. Work through them. Transform them into more helpful, healthier ideas that feel better. By doing so, you will be in a better position to handle whatever unfolds.

Perhaps you are doubting your ability to meet the challenges of your crisis. Maybe you have some regrets about things you've done or didn't do.

Select one negative, unhelpful, or unhealthy thought that is currently on your mind. Work through the following process:

1. Consider the Costs of This Thought

Let say you catch yourself thinking, "I'm going to lose my job."

What is the toll of this sentiment? It's demotivating. It's depressing. It diminishes the energy you have for your work and for other things as well. It makes you cranky. It's unpleasant for your co-workers. It leaks fear on your family.

> ACTIVITY
>
> Journal about the thought you've chosen.
>
> - How does it affect you?
> - What does it cost you?
> - What impact does it have on those around you?

2. Curtail the Inherent Emotional Charge

Take some slow, deep breaths. Take a few minutes to work through the techniques we discussed to dispel negative emotions and relax and release the tension. You can find them on p. 37.

3. Reframe This Thought without Absolutes

There's a tendency for most people to frame negative thoughts in dire, exaggerated terms. If something doesn't happen the way we want it, we moan that it will "never, ever" happen and that "everyone" will think less of us for the rest of our lives. Some small aspect of a project goes awry and we think the entire enterprise is doomed. Doomed, I say. Doomed!

Does your negative thought include absolute terms such as "always" or "never" or "everyone?" If so, stop and rephrase it to be more accurate. For example, "I'm going to lose my job" is more truthfully written as "I'm concerned I might lose my job."

TECHNIQUE
Rephrase for Accuracy

Pay attention to the words you use. When you utter absolute terms like "always", "never", and "everybody", immediately rephrase your statement to be more accurate.

---

4. Dispute It

Is this negative thought really true? What evidence is there to the contrary?

Identify facts that dispute the negative thought. The more counterarguments you can produce, the better.

For example, the thought "I'm going to lose my job" could be disputed with facts such as:

I don't know for sure that I will lose my job. Maybe I will, maybe I won't.

Yes, many people have lost their jobs but that doesn't mean I will.

I have valuable skills and experience. I am an asset to the company.

Similarly, if you have regrets about something you did or didn't do before your crisis began—if you are harboring any "Coulda Woulda Shoulda" thoughts, you can counter them with statements like:

I did the best I could with the knowledge and understanding I had at the time.

There is no way to go back in time. There is no way to change what happened (or didn't happen) in the past. I understand that what's done is done.

I have learned what I would do differently, going forward. There will be future opportunities for me to use what I've learned.

TECHNIQUE
Dispute The Unhelpful Thought

Dispute your negative thought. What evidence is there to the contrary?

Write out as many ways to refute it as you can.

---

5. Generate at Least Three Alternatives

Counter your negative thought by thinking of at least three alternative ways of looking at it.

By examining other ways to view the situation, you are likely to generate thoughts that are easier to bear. They may be neutral. They might even be positive. They are likely to give you a sense of relief. To the extent possible, aim for an alternative that feels better.

For example, if you are reaching for thoughts that feel better than "I'm going to lose my job," you might consider the following alternatives:

I'm grateful to have a job, especially when so many people don't.

As long as I am employed, I'll focus on doing the best work I can.

If I lose my job, I'll handle it. I will find new work.

If I do lose my job, I might be out of work temporarily, but it won't be forever.

If I do lose my job, I will explore new opportunities. I'll be open to finding work I'd rather do.

TECHNIQUE
Generate Alternatives

Going forward, whenever you notice a negative thought, pause. Generate at least three alternatives. Aim for "neutral" or "accurate."

Produce at least one thought that feels better.

IDENTIFY AND IMPLEMENT HEALTHY DISTRACTIONS

Just as distractions are helpful to dispel negative emotions, they are an effective way to curtail your thoughts during stressful times of uncertainty.

Take breaks from thinking about your crisis. In what helpful, healthy ways can you distract yourself?

There is a good reason jigsaw puzzles were such a hot commodity during the pandemic. Many people found they provided a pleasant, engaging way to occupy their overloaded brains. It was much more enjoyable to be focused on finding edge pieces than to be mulling over coronavirus concerns.

The best distractions engage your busy brain. For example, Peter has found that mowing his lawn doesn't prevent his mind from dwelling on his worries. But books do. Reading occupies his brain and shifts his attention from his troubles to beautiful places, clever, engaging characters and intriguing plots. Annie finds that arts and crafts work well for her. She gets so wrapped up in making things that she loses track of time. It's a relief to be absorbed in creative outlets, rather than fretting about her health.

Taking any positive action will feel better. It feels good to make a contribution. It's a relief to take steps to counter the situation. Helping others is a highly effective way to get your mind off your own concerns.

What about you? What are pleasant, healthy ways you might engage your mind to distract yourself from your crisis? How could you help others?

Also, be aware of activities that would be ineffective or unhealthy for you. Mowing doesn't occupy Peter's mind sufficiently, for example.

In contrast, surfing the internet sure is engaging for him—but it is not healthy or effective! It stresses him out and it is addictive. It's a distraction he must do his best to limit or avoid.

ACTIVITY

1. What are pleasant, healthy, engaging ways you might distract yourself during your crisis?
2. What could you be doing for others?
3. What activities would be ineffective or unhealthy for you? What should you limit or avoid?

◆

DISRUPT NEGATIVE THINKING LOOPS

Do you have a tendency to latch onto a negative thought and mull it over and over and over again? Or to fixate on an unpleasant occurrence—for example, mentally replaying an upsetting conversation over and over. (*Ugh! I should have said X or Y or Z at the meeting! X or Y or Z! Why didn't I say X or Y or Z?*)

If so, is this part of your response to your crisis? *I don't want to be evicted! I don't want to be evicted! I don't want to be evicted*

The danger here is that a repetitive negative thought can etch a wear-worn groove in your thinking. It can foster fear, stress, and a self-defeating attitude.

Thankfully, these are only thoughts. Just as you have the power to create them, you have the power to disrupt them and/or change them using the techniques presented in this chapter.

If you find yourself fixated on a negative thought, repeating it over and over in your head, try the following technique.

TECHNIQUE
Disrupt Negative Thinking Loops

---

1. Interrupt your thought pattern.
    - Say "enough!" out loud. Hold your hand up like a stop sign. (This may even make you giggle, which can break the loop.)
    - Change your body posture (for example, stand up if you are seated). If possible, change your physical location.
    - Take a few deep, slow conscious breaths.
2. Process and transform your thoughts.
    - Write down the repeating thought.
    - Rephrase for accuracy (p. 75).
    - Dispute it (p. 76).
    - Generate at least three alternatives (p. 77).
    - Pick a thought—any thought—that feels better. Write it out ten times. Say it out loud. Put a tune to it and sing it. Get your brain hooked on the new thought.
3. Distract yourself. Engage in something to give your mind something else to do (p. 78).

4. For the next day or so, wear a thick elastic band on your wrist. Whenever your negative thought recurs, snap the elastic. It will hurt (briefly) and will immediately interrupt the loop. It may seem odd but if you do this for a few days, you will train your brain to avoid this thought.

In times of crisis, one of the most effective ways to manage your mind is to engage it in taking action. That's the focus of the next chapter.

CHAPTER 5

Take Action

There may be much out of your control during your crisis. What isn't? What actions can you take to improve your experience of the situation? We've already covered steps you can take for your safety and well-being (Chapter 2), things you can do to handle your emotions (Chapter 3), and to manage your thoughts (Chapter 4).

What else can you do?

ACTIVITY

Make a list of possible courses of action you could take at this time. *Actually write (or type) out your options.* Consider:

- Steps you could take to improve your current situation
- Actions you could take to address a challenge
- Things you could do to help others
- Activities you enjoy

Now choose something on your list and do it. Taking action is one of the most effective ways to cope with stressful, uncertain circumstances. As soon as you start doing something, you are likely to feel relief.

However, if you are overwhelmed by your crisis, it may be difficult to get yourself going. You many procrastinate or avoid doing things that you know would be beneficial. If you are stuck, be kind and gentle with yourself. Give yourself the downtime you need. When you are ready to take action, here are some tips to help:

1. Do Less

When besieged by uncertain circumstances, we tend to take on too many things. We flounder and flail. Our actions are scattered so that not much of anything gets done. Our minds are going in multiple directions at once, which amplifies stress and anxiety.

Do less. Prune your *To Do* list. Set reasonable, achievable expectations. Begin with the basics. What are the two or three most important things to be done right now?

ACTIVITY

1. Review your list of possible actions. Circle your top two or three priorities.
2. Choose your top priority from among the items you've circled. Underline it. If in doubt, select whatever would be easiest for you at this time.
3. What would it mean to you if you would make progress on this priority? How would it feel?
4. How could you get started? What small, concrete steps could you take today to begin?

2. Focus on Starting

You don't have to finish. You don't have to get a certain amount done. Make your only objective to begin the task you have chosen.

Start.

Please do the next activity right now. (Yes, really.)

ACTIVITY

Select one single thing you could to do improve your current situation. Set a timer for ten minutes. Begin your chosen task.

How did you do? If you started, great! You are taking concrete steps to move forward. Know that whenever you get stuck, you just need to start something—anything—to get yourself moving again. A body at rest stays at rest. A body in motion keeps moving.

If you didn't take action, please try again. You owe it to yourself to take action. There is no point reading further until you can begin.

3. Do One Thing at a Time

Focus your full attention and your actions on only one activity at a time. Avoid multitasking.

It doesn't matter how many projects, activities, and ideas you are juggling. At a given instant, you can only do one thing.

"Oh no, not me," you may insist. "I'm a multi-tasker. Right now, while I'm reading this, I'm also making soup, listening to the news, and texting my mom."

You may believe you are doing several things simultaneously but studies have shown that's not possible. Really what happens is that your brain toggles among those different activities every second or so. At any given instant, you are doing only one of them. Every time you switch tasks, there is a cognitive cost as your brain switches gears. (*Now where was I again?*) By toggling so quickly among different activities, you're not doing any of them particularly well. Research has proven that multi-taskers reduce their productivity by about 40 per cent. 40 per cent!

Frankly, you're being unnecessarily hard on yourself. It's much easier to focus on one thing at a time. And here's the good news: when you stop trying to do everything at the same instant—when you focus on just one activity at a time—you will get more done, faster, more easily, with less stress.

Just do one thing at time. Give the task your full attention. When you conclude one activity, select your next task and do it. The more you can limit your focus to one and only one thing at a time, the better.

4. Minimize Distractions

If you find it difficult to concentrate, take a moment to identify and curtail whatever distractions are interfering with your attention. Are you easily sidetracked by any notifications of new emails or new social media posts? Are people around you interrupting your progress?

I understand! As I am writing this, I'm hearing weird scratching sounds in the attic, my dogs are whining for attention, and my husband just popped in to ask me to help him find a clipboard.

Of course, it's impossible to eliminate *all* distractions *all* the time. But to the extent you can *reduce* distractions—especially the siren calls of the internet and social media—the more you will reap the benefits of focusing on one thing at a time. Turn your phone ringer off when you can. Leave email alone until it's time to focus on only that, ideally only once or twice a day. Post a sign on your office door to notify your kids that you are unavailable unless someone is bleeding or on fire.

> ACTIVITY
>
> 1. What distractions are you experiencing? Make a list.
> 2. For each item on your list, brainstorm ways you might avoid, limit, reduce, or minimize it.

5. Break Projects and Activities into Baby Steps

If you can split your projects and activities into smaller pieces, the more manageable—and achievable—they become. This is especially important during a crisis when everyday activities can seem daunting.

Be kind to yourself.

Take your top priority. How could you break it up into tiny, easy tasks? If your top priority is to find a job, for example, you could break that into smaller tasks such as "update my resume", "look up job postings", "make a list of contacts I should talk to", "call each person on my list", "seek what job search and career counseling resources are available to me", and so forth.

Ideally, baby steps should be ridiculously small—so small you don't think twice about doing them. If "update my resume" seems too overwhelming, break it up into yet smaller pieces. (E.g., "read my old resume", "add any new or missing information", "ask people I trust to read my resume and make suggestions for improvement", etc.)

> ACTIVITY
>
> Consider the task that is your top priority. How could you break it into baby steps? What are the smallest actions you could take to move forward?

6. Monitor and Reward Your Progress

You are undergoing a crisis. Be kind to yourself. Praise yourself for whatever you get done. Bonus points if you can give yourself treats or otherwise reward yourself.

Give yourself credit for any forward movement. You updated you resume? Pat yourself on the back! Can you give yourself a treat? Maybe take a moment to savor a cup of coffee?

What would be easy ways to acknowledge and reward your efforts?

> ACTIVITY
>
> Consider the task that is your top priority. How could keep track of progress towards your goals? How could you reward yourself?

7. Focus on What *Is* Getting Done, Rather Than What *Isn't*

It is highly gratifying and much more pleasant to acknowledge your accomplishments than to despair over everything you have yet to do.

Sorry, but you will never get it all done. There will always be things left to do. Avoid judging yourself. Counter false, unhelpful thoughts such as "I should be doing more." You are doing the best you can, under challenging circumstances. If you were able to do more, you would.

Creativity author Julia Cameron recommends a daily practice of creating a "Ta Dah" list: Take a few moments each evening to write down everything you did in the day—big and small. For example: *I showered. I got dressed. I fed the dogs. I made breakfast. I savored my coffee. I brushed and flossed. I wrote a chapter despite distractions. I found my husband's clipboard.*

Why not give it a try? Especially if you are feeling less productive than you were before your crisis began.

HELPFUL DAILY PRACTICE
Make a "TA DAH" List

At the end of the day, write down everything you did, big and small.

Give yourself credit for all forward progress in any area of life.

---

8. Avoid Comparing Yourself to Others

Focus on your own progress rather than bothering over what others seem to be doing. Avoid comparing yourself to others—especially posts on social media. Others may seem to be doing more than you but you don't have the full picture. You don't know for sure what others are truly experiencing

Sure, Kiki may be churning out gourmet meals every day but maybe cooking is about all she can do these days. Sure, she's eating well, but maybe her marriage is in a shambles, her home is a neglected mess, and she is worried about a strange looking mole on her arm.

Let others do what's important to them. Just focus on doing what's important to you in getting through your crisis.

9. Take Five-Minute Mini-Breaks

Mini-breaks (p. 56) provide an effective technique for reducing anxiety and managing your thoughts. It's also a great way to get things done. Especially during a time of crisis, it's essential to give your brain and body brief breaks throughout the day. If you don't—if you push yourself non-stop—you will burn out.

If you haven't given five-minute mini-breaks a try, please do. What would be healthy, helpful, peaceful five-minute mini-breaks for you?

What activities would be pleasant, peaceful, and a change from your current task? This will be unique to you and the task at hand. Writers need to take a break from sitting at the keyboard whereas gardeners need to rest their bodies. Parents may need some quiet time whereas kids may need to run around and burn off some energy.

On your mini-breaks, avoid any activity you find stressful, any multi-tasking (trying to cram umpteen things into your break), or anything difficult to stop after just five minutes (e.g., web-surfing).

◆

Taking action—any action—is pretty much guaranteed to make you feel better. You are more likely to feel that you are coping well with your crisis. As you contemplate the actions you can take, consider what you can do to make the best of your current situation. That's the focus of Chapter 6.

CHAPTER 6

Make the Best of the Situation

Once you have addressed the fundamentals (Chapter 2) and have found ways to handle your emotions (Chapter 3), manage your mind (Chapter 4), and take action (Chapter 5) during this challenging time, you have the option of doing more. If you wish, you can examine how to not just survive your current crisis—but thrive in it.

How might you make the best of the current circumstances? How could you take advantage of the time at hand? Take a moment to assess your present situation and to explore how you might spend this period. Make some deliberate decisions, then carry on accordingly.

This chapter presents a few ideas to get you started, but really there are infinite possibilities. I encourage you to devise and pursue your own plans.

Maybe you don't want to do a thing. No problem. But make that a conscious choice here and now. Actively decide to make this a period of prolonged downtime in which you focus on simply surviving. That's fine. That's different than if you were to passively surrender yourself to whatever is unfolding, without making any deliberate decisions, letting months drift by, until one day you find yourself thinking, "Darn! I should have done X! I could have used this time to do Y!"

To the extent that you *do* want to actively take steps to make the best of this situation, please continue reading.

Consider some of the ideas already covered in earlier chapters. If you wanted to, for example, you could use this period of time to:

- Catch up on your reading
- Engage in hobbies or personal pursuits
- Learn something new
- Connect with people you care about
- Help others

What else could you do to make the best of your current circumstances? For example, you could use this time in your life to:

- Identify opportunities in whatever is unfolding
- Make desired changes in your life
- Improve your relationships:
    - Strengthen important relationships
    - Resolve conflicts and resentment
    - Forgive
- Put things in order:
    - Identify priorities
    - Living space
    - Prune your belongings
    - Finances
    - Legal documents

Do any of these latter ideas appeal to you? If so, please turn to any sections that do. Otherwise, please proceed to the next chapter.

◆

IDENTIFY OPPORTUNITIES IN WHATEVER IS UNFOLDING

Any crisis creates opportunities. What prospects might there be for you these days? How could you make the best of the current situation?

Begin by thinking about your personal life. What opportunities might there be for your personal growth and development? For example, if you are someone who tends to worry, you could use this crisis as a way of dealing with your anxiety and finding better ways of responding to uncertain, uncontrollable circumstances.

What about your home life? Does the current situation give you extra motivation to change things around or to tackle a big project you've been putting off?

Might you use this time to interact with people you care about? Or to reflect back on the people in your past with whom you've lost touch?

Consider your professional life. Does this crisis spark ideas about new goods or services to offer? Or different ways of working? Are there practical improvements you could implement?

If you're not sure, do some research. Look online for ideas and inspiration.

Confer with relevant, trusted others. For example, you could brainstorm with your family about possible improvements to your home life. You might exchange ideas around with your favorite co-workers about possible opportunities on the job or in your field.

ACTIVITY

Brainstorm answers to the following questions.

- What new opportunities are there in your personal life?
- What new opportunities are there in your home life?
- What new social opportunities might there be?

- What new opportunities are there in your work life?
- What new business or financial opportunities might there be?

MAKE DESIRED CHANGES IN YOUR BEHAVIOR

Are there any changes you'd like to make in how you operate? Are there any behaviors you'd like to adjust? Any habits you'd like to establish? Any unhelpful patterns you'd like to disrupt?

If so, consider that the easiest time to make a lasting behavioral adjustment is during a time of major change. For example, if you are moving to a new city, it's relatively easy to quit smoking in your new location because you won't have any of the geographical or social cues to smoke that were embedded your former environment.

Similarly, any major crisis can offer a fresh start. "Normal" social cues and triggers might be disrupted. One possible benefit of this is that, going forward, you get to choose how you'd like to proceed.

ACTIVITY

1. Clear a few minutes to write (or type) out answers to the following questions:
   - What's working well in your life? What's not? What adjustments would you like to make, going forward?
   - Which of your current behaviors and activities are healthy and helpful? What are you doing that feels good?
   - What would you like to do more of?
   - What are you not doing that you would like to begin doing?
   - Which of your current behaviors are unhelpful and/or unhealthy? What are you doing that doesn't feel good?
   - What would you like to do less of? What are you doing that you would like to reduce, limit, or cease doing?

2. Review your answers. Which of these items are most important to you? Which would have the biggest, best impact on your life? Circle your priorities.

Choose one item to begin implementing. What needs to happen? How can you make it happen? What is in place to support you? What small actions can you take this week?

If in doubt, identify the simplest, easiest step you could take to move forward. Baby steps are especially helpful in making personal changes.

If your goal is to establish a habit of walking at least an hour a day, say, then you might begin the process by committing to walk at least ten minutes a day (assuming that sounds realistic for you). After that becomes second nature, aim for fifteen. When that seems like old hat, go for twenty...until eventually you increase your total daily walking time to an hour.

The key here is that your beginning goal should be so easy it's laughable. Going back to the last example, if walking ten minutes a day is easy as pie, that's a great place to start. If, however, it proves to be too challenging, then start with five minutes. Still too much? Begin with one or two.

It *really* doesn't matter where you start, as long as you (a) begin, and (b) keep moving towards your desired destination. Any small forward progress is a step towards your goal.

Baby steps work in reverse, too. Let's say you want to reduce or eliminate an unhelpful or unhealthy habit. Small changes can have big impact.

You can find a way of reducing your bad habit incrementally. For example, if you're a pack a day smoker, that's twenty cigarettes a day. It probably wouldn't be difficult to cut your consumption down to nineteen cigarettes a day this week, right? If that's easy, then next week, you could reduce your daily habit to eighteen... and so on.

For example, if you are surfing the internet excessively, begin by measuring just how much time you are spending online. Then you could aim to reduce that by, say 5% for a day or two. Then you could reduce it by another 5%.

Aim for steady progress in your desired direction.

◆

IMPROVE YOUR RELATIONSHIPS

During times of crisis, people pull together. Consider that your crisis may provide an opportunity to reach out and connect with people you care about.

STRENGTHEN IMPORTANT RELATIONSHIPS

Which of your relationships would you like to improve? Consider friends, family, co-workers, neighbors, and anyone whose company you enjoy.

Think back over your life—your childhood, your teens, your early adulthood up to now. As you think of each life chapter, who was special to you? Is there anyone from your past you miss? Why not reach out to them?

How can you deepen your bonds with the people you care most about? How can you show them your affection? How can you reveal what they mean to you?

ACTIVITY

1. Make a list of your most important relationships, past and present.
2. Beside each name, jot down one or more things you could to do strengthen or deepen your connection.

RESOLVE CONFLICTS AND RESENTMENTS

Are there people with whom you have unresolved grudges, resentments, or conflicts? Against the scale of your current crisis, are your past quarrels substantial enough to hold onto? If you choose to, you can use the current situation as an opportunity to find peace, make amends, and let go of grudges.

Begin by identifying anyone with whom you have a current conflict and anyone with whom you are holding a grudge from the past. What small, easy actions can you take to improve things between the two of you? What small shifts in thought, word, or attitude would improve the situation?

ACTIVITY

1. Make a list of the people with whom you have current or past unresolved issues.
2. Beside each name, jot down one or more things you could to do improve things between you.

Is there a challenging relationship in your life you'd like to improve? Your crisis might provide an opportunity to find a new way forward. Your perspectives and priorities might shift. If you'd like, you could explore possible ways to change your interactions.

ACTIVITY

1. Select one challenging relationship. Answers the following:
   - Why and how is this a challenging relationship?
   - How does this person interact with you?
   - How does this person interact with others?
   - What do you not like about this person?
   - Consider your own behavior. What do you do that is somewhat similar to the aspects of this other person that you don't like? *For example, if you find this person to be deceitful, ask, "In what ways am I being false, fake, or deceitful?"*
   - Re-read your answers to the above questions. Circle the harshest, most painful words. How can you change these words to be less negative and/or more accurate? E.g., *if you originally described the person as a "fake," you might re-write that word as"shielding their true self from some people, including me." If you originally described them as "ungrateful", you might re-phrase that as "unable to express appreciation to me".*
   - Identify (at least) three positive qualities of this person. *Bonus points for listing more.*
   - What do you have in common with this person?
   - How important is this relationship to you? Why?
   - What hopes do you have for this relationship? Describe the kind of relationship you would like to have with this person.
   - What fears do you have about this relationship?
   - What would it mean to you if you could improve this relationship?
   - To what extent is this person doing the best they can, given their current understanding, knowledge, and skills?
   - What's one tiny thing you can do shift your thoughts or attitudes about this person?
   - To what extent is acceptance required here (p. 40)?
   - What actions could you take to improve this relationship? To what extent is forgiveness required here? *(See the following section)*.

2. Whenever you know you'll be interacting with this person, review your answers. Circle any helpful insights. Take a few moments to contemplate the kind of relationship you would like to have with them. Allow it to happen.

FORGIVE

Regardless of how kind we try to be, each of us has been hurt by someone else—and each of us has hurt someone else. Just as we must apologize and ask forgiveness when we do wrong, it's only fair that we forgive those who wrong us.

Sometimes that's not easy. When someone hurts us, there is a natural resistance to responding with kindness. But forgiveness is not approval for what occurred. Forgiveness is not "letting someone off the hook." Forgiveness is an acknowledgment that we all make mistakes.

"But you don't understand," you may protest. "They were wrong! They hurt me badly! Why should I forgive them?" Well, ask yourself this: Would you rather be right or would you rather be healed? If you want to heal, you must forgive them.

Truthfully, forgiveness is letting YOU off the hook: it's a way to release the pain, the anger, the fear, and the resentment you experience when someone hurts you. Forgiveness gives you the opportunity to heal and move on.

The alternatives don't work. Lashing back or seeking revenge is never as satisfying as you imagine. Harsh actions injure you in the long run. Holding grudges and hard feelings against those who have harmed you hurts you much, much more than it affects them.

The longer you let resentments and regrets fester, the more you are damaging your own peace of mind. It's impossible to be happy if you are bearing burdens from the past. Who does it serve if you are walking around, bitter and seething about something that happened a decade ago…while the person who hurt you can't even remember your name, let alone the incident? Grudges hurt you, not them.

"But it's too late," you may say. No, it isn't. When you hurt someone, it's better to apologize immediately—but it's better to apologize late than not at all. Forgiveness works the same way. You can be way overdue when it comes to forgiving others. But as soon as you do, you can heal. Besides, you can't move forward until you forgive.

"But I don't even know where they are, what they're doing, if they are even alive," you might counter. It doesn't matter. If you can forgive someone in person, it's powerful. But you can also forgive someone without them knowing anything about it. It doesn't matter where they are or what they're doing—you have the power to forgive them, right here, right now.

Forgiveness is really a gift you give yourself. You'll feel the difference in your own heart when you truly forgive someone. There's a little shift, deep down. It feels like relief. It's the first step to replacing the pain of the incident with peace and joy.

Think of a specific time in which you were wronged. Someone did a bad thing. Now what are you going to do?

Option 1: you can stew—keep it all inside, festering. This only hurts you.

Option 2: you can play the victim. You tell everyone what a horrible thing happened to you and broadcast what a terrible person the perpetrator of the incident is. This only foments negativity and spreads the pain.

Option 3: you can lash back—seek revenge or payback. This may give you momentary satisfaction but it won't feel nearly as satisfying as you anticipate—and it will not heal your pain.

Option 4: you can forgive them and move on. If you want to heal, forgiveness is the answer.

If you have someone to forgive, consider using your crisis as an opportunity to do so. You can wipe the slate clean.

ACTIVITY

1. Choose one person you need to forgive. Answer the following questions
   - What is it costing you to hold these resentments?
   - How does it make you feel?
   - How does it affect how you are living your life?
   - What benefits might there be to forgiving them? How would you feel? How might it improve your life?
   - To what extent were they doing the best they could, given the skills, knowledge, and experience they had at the time?
2. Imagine this person as a child, helpless and alone. Could you have compassion for them in that circumstance? Can you acknowledge that they are a fallible human being, susceptible to making mistakes? You don't need to justify or approve of what they did. But can you forgive them?
3. Forgive them.

When you are ready, on another occasion, choose another person you need to forgive. Work through the process. Forgive them.

◆

PUT THINGS IN ORDER

Under normal circumstances, it's easy to put off those things that are important but not necessarily urgent. Things like revamping your living space or reviewing your finances or updating your will.

When something life-changing like a major crisis occurs, it can cause us to pause and rethink things. It can spark opportunities to take care of what is important in your life.

Identify key things in your life requiring stewardship. "Stewardship" is a stodgy sounding word yet a wonderful concept: stewardship means taking good and thoughtful care of something. It's a warmer, cozier, more competent way of approaching the many responsibilities in your life. Rather than thinking "Oh crap, I have to do X, Y, and Z!", it's a shift to calmly managing whatever comes up for the purpose of taking good care of what's important in your life.

Of what—or whom—do you want to be taking good care? Your relationships—personal and professional? Your home? Your family? Your finances? Something else? Answer thoughtfully and candidly.

Next consider how you might take better care of this person or thing.

If anything seems like a burden, how might you reframe it into more positive terms? For example, if your domestic responsibilities seem overwhelming, it might help to reframe your chores as taking good care of your home. "Ugh. I have to clean the kitchen. Again." becomes "I'm making my household cleaner and safer", "I'm taking good care of my family", or "I'm grateful to have a kitchen to clean."

ACTIVITY

1. Of what—or whom—do you want to be taking good care? Make a list.
2. For each item on your list, brainstorm how can you take better care of this person or thing.
   - Does this seem like a burden? If so, how might you reframe it into more positive terms?

PUT YOUR LIVING SPACE IN ORDER

What do you love about your home? What do you not?

What's one thing you could do to improve where you live? How could you make it more comfortable or functional or appealing to you?

In what ways is your home meeting your current needs and activities? In what ways is it not? For example, if you work from home, you may need to find ways to separate your "work" space from your "home" areas. Perhaps you'd like to carve out a private corner as your personal retreat.

It may be that your priorities have shifted, as a result of your crisis.

Perhaps that fancy coffee maker you've been coveting doesn't seem to be so important. Maybe you weren't very fussy about domestic messes a few months ago...but now you are more motivated to keep everything spic and span.

What aspects of your living space would you like to give some attention, going forward?

ACTIVITY

1. Walk around your living space with paper and pen (or tablet). In each room or area, ask yourself the following questions:
   - What's working well for you in this space?
   - What's not?
   - What looks good?
   - What doesn't?
   - What needs attention or repair?
2. After you've surveyed your space, review your notes. What would you most like to address? Circle your number one priority.
3. What's the simplest, easiest thing you could do to move forward on your top priority?
4. Do it. Take action to improve your living space.

PRUNE YOUR BELONGINGS

Much of what we own is unimportant "stuff". A crisis can shift your priorities. Given what is going on, you can view your belongings with fresh eyes. What are you holding onto that you don't really need?

Are you holding on to supplies you might need "someday" but haven't touched in years? Have you been lugging around books that really aren't that important to you? Does your closet hold items that don't fit or don't flatter or don't get worn in your present life? Are you hanging onto items others have given you that you don't really need or want...but you feel guilty about getting rid of them?

If that sounds like you, you can use your crisis to get rid of:

- Things you don't need
- Things you don't like
- Things you aren't using
- Things that make you feel guilty or otherwise icky
- Things you're holding onto because they might be useful "someday"
- Things that need repair—that you are unlikely to fix
- Clothes that don't fit or aren't flattering
- Things you want to give to someone "someday." Why not give them now?

Give yourself a gift by jettisoning your excess belongings. The less you hang onto, the more space and freedom you'll have. And the more your living space will reflect the current "you" and your revised priorities. What can you sell? What can you give to people who will put it to better use? What can you donate to charity?

Only hold onto:

- Things you love
- Things that make you feel good
- Things you use
- Things in good repair (or that you commit to repair within the next month)
- Things that fit you well and look good on you

ACTIVITY

1. Designate three cardboard boxes as "donate/charity", "give to specific people", and "sell". Put them beside a large garbage can.
2. Walk around your living space. Find at least ten items that belong in these receptacles. Distribute them accordingly.

If you are daunted by the idea of pruning your belongings, start small. Choose the smallest, easiest space to purge. Get rid of what you don't need. See how the experience feels. If it seems helpful, carry on with other areas of your home.

ACTIVITY

1. Pick the easiest possible space to purge—a sock drawer, a cupboard, the bathroom, wherever. Remove all the contents. As you do so, get rid of what you don't need. Give it away, throw it away, sell it—do what makes sense to get it out of your space. If in doubt, you don't need it. It's just "stuff." When you put the remaining items back, organize them neatly.
2. Make a list of the rooms or areas in your living space.
3. On another occasion, repeat the first activity, focusing on a different room or area.
4. Repeat this process until you've worked your way through every area in your home. *Maybe you tackle one room a month or one drawer or cupboard per week—find a schedule that works for you so that you*

can go through your entire living space this year. Jettison what you don't need.

Bonus Activity: set up an ongoing system by which you will keep clutter at bay. *(Heidi has a "one in—one out" rule. If she buys something new, she gets rid of something old. James keeps "give/donate" boxes handy to prune his belongings throughout the year. Pat schedules an annual spring cleaning/purge to go through the family's entire living space.)* What will work for you?

PUT YOUR FINANCES IN ORDER

Does thinking about money cause you anxiety and dread? Do you avoid dealing with financial matters?

To the extent you can overcome that resistance, you have the opportunity to examine your current finances and make choices about the future

Begin with the basics. What is your monthly income? What are your assets? What resources do you have available? What are your expenses? What challenges do you need to solve? What adjustments are needed, going forward?

What is most pressing? What is most important to you at this point in time?

If you're not sure, take the time to examine how you are currently spending your money. Pull out your financial information for the past two months. Tally up how much money you have spent on what kinds of things. Tailor your assessment to make sense for your unique life situation. Create categories that make sense for you *(e.g., work, home, personal, food, pets, entertainment, learning, leisure, health and dental, travel, or whatever else is relevant).*

After you crunch the numbers, answer the following:

- On what are you spending more money than expected?
- On what are you spending less money than expected?
- What adjustments would you like to make in how you spend your money? Brainstorm options and solutions.

Do you need to find new or greater sources of income? What are your options? Do you have goods or services to barter? Is there anything you can sell?

Do you need to economize? What can you trim from your expenses? What can you reduce? What can you eliminate? Were you planning a big purchase that can be postponed or canceled?

If you need financial relief, ask for it. This is not a time to be proud or shy or to play the victim, waiting for someone else to swoop in and save you. You can't get help unless you take action. Make the phone calls. Fill in the forms. Apply for available assistance. Inquire about payment deferrals, reductions, and refinancing.

Look for creative solutions. For example, if you've lost your job, ask your landlord for a rent reduction or deferral. Many property owners would much rather get less money—or get their rent later—than lose good tenants.

Once you get a handle on your fiscal priorities, look at how your financial information is set up and organized. Do your loved ones have the numbers and passwords they need, should something happen to you?

When Irene's husband surprised her with a request for a divorce after twenty years of marriage, she was stunned. Besides the emotional and social upheaval, she found herself in a financial mess. Her spouse had taken care of all their finances throughout her marriage. She didn't know where their accounts and assets were, let alone practicalities like passwords. She was essentially destitute and entirely at the mercy of a person intent on cutting her out of his life.

Karl was in a similar bind when his wife died unexpectedly. She had been their household's financial manager...and he had a tough time convincing credit card companies, financial institutions, and service providers to allow him access to their accounts.

"The phone company would not allow me to even make inquiries into our account because my name wasn't on it," he said. "It was a costly, stressful, time-consuming mess to sort everything out."

ACTIVITY

If you have a domestic partner, do this together: make a list of all your household's financial accounts and service providers as well as how to access them.

To the extent possible, put both of your names on every account. Keep this list in a safe, secure location and update it with any changes, as they occur.

PUT YOUR LEGAL PAPERWORK IN ORDER

When my mother passed away unexpectedly, the greatest gift she gave me was that her legal paperwork was accurate, complete, and up to date. Her wishes were crystal clear. It's hard to think straight when you're grieving, so having everything spelled out was a relief. Having all the paperwork in order also saved me the expense, stress, and emotional toll of probate, legal wrangling, and tax hell.

Julia was not so fortunate. Sorting out her mother's estate required a year of hemorrhaging money for legal fees and taxes—

plus grappling with a mountain of indecipherable paperwork and umpteen stressful meetings.

"It was so emotionally draining," she said. "Every meeting with the lawyer meant we had to relive Mom's death. A half hour probate meeting would knock me out for the rest of the day."

Sid had it worse: when his parents died, the surviving family members squabbled over the estate.

"I can't believe it happened in my own family," he lamented. "It was so unpleasant and such a cliché. It was so bad I haven't spoken to my own sister in five years."

What kind of experience do you want for the people you care about?

Yes, this can be a morbid, scary topic. But it's important. It behooves you to put things in order for the people important to you.

If you haven't already done so, consider using your crisis as an impetus to update your legal documents including your will, your medical wishes, and your funerary wishes.

Decide who you want to make legal, financial, and/or medical decisions for you, should you become incapacitated. What conversations do you need to have with them now so your wishes are clear?

Who needs to have access to what information?

What is a secure process and location to keep key financial and legal information so that it is safe from scammers and yet accessible to the key people you've chosen to manage things for you?

ACTIVITY

1. Identify who you want—and who you don't want—to make legal, financial, and/or medical decisions for you, going forward. Under what circumstances?
2. Who needs access to what information?
3. With this in mind, review and organize your legal documents including your will, your medical wishes, and your funerary wishes.
   - What's in place already?
   - What gaps need to be addressed?
4. Take the necessary steps to ensure all your legal documents are accurate and complete. Compile key logistical and financial information such as accounts and passwords.
5. Devise a safe process and place to secure your important legal and financial information.
6. Inform relevant people about your wishes and the logistics to carry them out.

CHAPTER 7

Dealing with Ongoing or Long-term Crises

Some crises are relatively brief—a few days or weeks of challenges, and then things resolve. Many more crises unfold over a longer time frame. Often, they are ongoing with no concrete end in sight. These longer-term crises require strength, patience, and the application of every coping technique in this book.

When Mike's brain tumors were detected, neither he nor his wife could have predicted the journey they would take as they navigated various medical facilities and treatments over the next few years. They left the "forever home" they'd so painstakingly renovated, relocating to a new house in different state. They never knew how much time they would have left together, but they knew it wouldn't be enough.

During any long-term crisis there are "good days" and "not-so-good" days. There are some beautiful moments, and some unpleasant occurrences. There are opportunities and challenges.

There's a grappling with the unknown, in terms of general worries *(How long will this go on? How on earth will it resolve? Will my life ever go back to normal?)* as well as practical concerns *(How will I pay the rent next month? Which course of treatment is best for me? Is it time for hospice?)*

Ongoing crises can be exhausting, both physically and mentally. As more and more time goes by, you can feel more and more fatigued, drained, and worn down. There can be a tendency to lose faith in whatever it unfolding. To despair. To sink into negative thinking.

The ongoing stress of long-term challenges can manifest as irritability, mood swings, difficulty concentrating, or feeling overwhelmed. It can cause disrupted sleep or oversleeping. It can trigger obsessive or compulsive behaviors, addictions, or emotional eating.

Unchecked over time, chronic stress can cause physical ailments such as teeth grinding and fractures, headaches, skin rashes, acne, hair loss, back pain, gastrointestinal problems, heart disease, high blood pressure, chest pain, irregular heartbeat, infertility, or weight gain. During the Covid-19 pandemic, for example, as the months dragged on, dentists and doctors reported a surge in stress-related ailments.

People experience chronic stress in different ways. What have you noticed in your own experience? It is helpful to recognize how it manifests in your body and behavior.

ACTIVITY

If you are going through an ongoing or long-term crisis, take a few minutes to journal about how it is affecting you.

1. How do you feel, physically? Scan each part of your body. Describe what you sense in your body in as much detail as you can.
2. Are you experiencing any recent physical ailments?
3. Describe your current mental state. How do you feel psychologically?
4. What thoughts are foremost in your mind these days?
5. Describe your current energy level (physical and mental).
6. What toll is this situation taking on you?
7. How is it affecting the people around you?

When you are undergoing a long-term crisis, it is important to recognize how chronic stress manifests in you so you can take steps to deal with it. For example, if you notice that you are grinding your teeth, you can use a mouth guard, practice daily relaxation techniques, and consult with your dentist.

When Marie is under stress, she's irritable and prone to compulsive eating. She's in a constant state of worry. She sleeps ten hours a night. If the stress persists unabated—if she fails to find healthy ways to interrupt these patterns—her symptoms escalate: her arms break out in ugly sores.

"It's like my body is sending out a super vivid alarm," she says. "It's a signal I need to immediately find ways to calm myself."

Mini-meditations and slow breathing work well for Marie—when she remembers to do them. In periods of chronic stress, however, she "forgets". When she realizes what's happening, she sets alarms on her phone to cue herself to pause for a few minutes to decompress, several times a day.

Think about how chronic stress manifests in you. What are the early warning signs? What are the more severe symptoms that can arise? What do you need to be on the lookout for?

ACTIVITY

Recall past challenging times in your life.

1. What were the initial physical signs of stress that you noticed?
2. What did you do to alleviate these initial symptoms of stress?
3. Have you experienced more severe symptoms of stress? Describe what happened. How did your body react under long-term stress? What did you do about it? What helped? What didn't?
4. Going forward, be on the lookout for these physical signs and symptoms of stress. Whenever they start to manifest, apply what you know works for you to reduce stress.

You are the expert on you. You know how your body and brain react to stress. You know what alleviates your symptoms and what makes them worse. In times of long-term or ongoing crises, however, it can be challenging to apply what you know about yourself.

If you get stuck, consider the tools and techniques in the earlier chapters of this book, which are presented below as a checklist. As you read the list, put a star beside any that you know work well for you.

Check any other items you would like to implement. Feel free to re-read any sections that seem particularly helpful or appealing.

COPING SKILLS CHECKLIST

1. Tend to the Basics (Chapter 2)

- ☐ Control what you can
- ☐ Suspend self-judgment
- ☐ Address your fundamental human needs:
    - ☐ Maximize your safety
    - ☐ Practice good self-care
    - ☐ Attend to your physical needs:
        - ☐ Practise good body maintenance
        - ☐ Get outdoors
        - ☐ Move your body every day
        - ☐ Foster good sleep
        - ☐ Take care of your psychological needs:
        - ☐ Make your mental health a priority
        - ☐ Give your brain regular breaks
        - ☐ Occupy your mind

- ☐ Nourish your mind
- ☐ Acquire the information you need

☐ Address your spiritual needs:

- ☐ Nourish your spirit
- ☐ Seek solace and strength in your spiritual beliefs

☐ Attend to your social needs:

- ☐ Suspend judgment of others
- ☐ Connect with people
- ☐ Find support
- ☐ Help others

2. Handle Your Emotions (Chapter 3)

- ☐ Examine your feelings
- ☐ Dispel strong emotions
- ☐ Manage any sadness and grief
- ☐ Deal with any anger
- ☐ Reduce any fear and anxiety:
  - ☐ Understand that whatever happens, you'll handle it
  - ☐ Recognize the futility of worry
  - ☐ Take action
  - ☐ Distract yourself
  - ☐ Scan your body
  - ☐ Consider EFT tapping
  - ☐ Fake it 'til you make it
- ☐ Reduce stress and cultivate calm:
  - ☐ Reduce unnecessary stressors
  - ☐ Take breaks
  - ☐ Scrutinize your technology
  - ☐ Unplug
  - ☐ Spend time in nature
  - ☐ Meditate

- ☐ Focus on the current moment

3. Manage Your Mind (Chapter 4)

- ☐ Cultivate positive thoughts:
  - ☐ Keep track of good thoughts
  - ☐ Look for the good in the situation
  - ☐ Savor special moments throughout your day
  - ☐ Practice daily gratitude
  - ☐ Appreciate the people and things you may have been undervaluing
  - ☐ Search for different perspectives and new thoughts that feel better
  - ☐ Carry some good thoughts with you
- ☐ Counter negative thoughts:
  - ☐ Consider the costs of this thought
  - ☐ Curtail the inherent emotional charge
  - ☐ Reframe the thought without absolutes
  - ☐ Dispute it
  - ☐ Generate at least three alternative thoughts
- ☐ Identify and implement healthy distractions
- ☐ Disrupt negative thinking loops

4. Take Action (Chapter 5)

- ☐ Do less
- ☐ Focus on starting
- ☐ Do one thing at a time
- ☐ Minimize distractions
- ☐ Break projects and activities into baby steps
- ☐ Monitor and reward your progress
- ☐ Focus on what *is* getting done, rather than what *isn't*
- ☐ Avoid comparing yourself to others

- ☐ Take five-minute mini-breaks

5. Make the Best of the Situation (Chapter 6)

- ☐ Identify opportunities in whatever is unfolding
- ☐ Make desired changes in your life
- ☐ Improve your relationships:
  - ☐ Strengthen important relationships
  - ☐ Resolve conflicts and resentments
  - ☐ Forgive
- ☐ Put things in order:
  - ☐ Identify priorities
  - ☐ Living space
  - ☐ Prune your belongings
  - ☐ Finances
  - ☐ Legal documents

ACTIVITY

1. Read the Coping Skills Checklist. As you do:
   - Put a star beside any items that you know work well for you
   - Put a check mark beside any other items you would like to try
2. Review the items you've marked on the preceding list. Of these, what are the simplest, easiest things you could implement today? Circle them.
3. Implement what you've circled.

CHAPTER 8

Navigating the Unknown Future

You are undergoing a time of crisis. It's unclear how things will unfold.

This chapter is presented as a self-guided workshop to prepare you for your unknown future. To get the most out it, please write (or type) out your responses.

Depending on the nature of your crisis, it might make sense to involve other people in this process. Couples, families, or business partners may wish to collaborate. If so, have each person do each of the activities individually, then come together to share answers and brainstorm collective ideas for going forward.

◆

EXAMINE LESSONS LEARNED

There are opportunities to learn and grow from every experience. No matter what we go through, we can gain new wisdom, knowledge, and insights.

This is particularly true when we encounter a major challenge or change. We can learn a lot when we move to a new home or a new job or a new chapter in life. We can see our lives in a fresh way. We can shift our perspectives and expectations. We can gain an enhanced understanding of how we operate and how the world works.

The bigger the challenge or change, the greater the potential lessons inherent in the experience.

Your crisis provides an opportunity to learn and grow.

Contemplate your experiences—big and small—during your crisis. What have you learned? What have you observed?

ACTIVITY

Journal about your experiences during your crisis:

- What have you noticed about yourself?
- What have you found out about your family and friends?
- What have you discovered about your community?
- What have you learned about the world?
- What do you see differently now than you did before?
- What lessons have you learned?

Next, broaden your perspective a bit to examine the implications and consequences of your crisis. Contemplate the transformations you've seen. Which changes do you expect to be temporary? What will be more long-lasting? What new modifications are likely to arise?

ACTIVITY

1. What changes have you already witnessed in your life as a result of your crisis? Consider any of the following:

    - Your personal life
    - Your professional life
    - Your home life
    - Your social life
    - Your health and fitness
    - Your leisure pursuits

2. Imagine that it is two years from today:
   - What do you foresee?
   - What aspects of life do you expect to go back to the way they were?
   - Which are likely to remain altered?
   - What subsequent changes might there be?

One key to navigating your unknown future is to understand, going into it, your real values and priorities. If you know what's truly important to you, you will be better equipped to make good decisions and take appropriate actions, no matter what happens.

◆

IDENTIFY YOUR VALUES

Your values reveal your personal ideals, your guiding principles, and your inner code of conduct. These can shift over time as you get older, as you experience life, and as you undergo new circumstances. Please take a moment to identify what is most important to you now—at this point in time.

Read the following list of words and phrases (adapted from the *Life Values Self-Assessment Test).* Circle five that are the most important to you today.

Community	Friendship	Location	Prestige
Creativity	Health	Loyalty	Security
Enjoyment	Independence	Personal Accomplishment	Service
Expertness	Integrity	Personal Development	Spirituality
Family	Justice	Power	Wealth
	Leadership		Wisdom

What do you notice about what you've circled? Any surprises? Has your crisis shifted priorities for you?

ACTIVITY

Give some thought to each item you circled, one at a time.

- How has this value manifested in your life? How has it affected you?
- How is this value being shown during your crisis? How is it affecting your current experiences?
- How might this value help or direct you in the uncertain future?

Going forward, keep your key values in mind to guide your actions and decisions. Think of them as your "through-line." That's a term coined by theatre legend Konstantin Stanislavski (creator of "method acting"). He encouraged actors to think beyond the particular scene they were in—to understand their character's underlying motivation throughout the entire play. By considering the bigger picture, actors can bring greater depth and authenticity to any given scene.

You can do the same thing in real life. If you understand that your personal through-line is "justice" for example, you can apply it to every situation you experience. You can use it as your personal North Star to guide your choices and priorities, no matter what you encounter.

◆

EVALUATE YOUR PRIORITIES

Think back to a time before your crisis began. What were your key goals then? What were your major challenges then?

ACTIVITY

1. Identify a time just before your crisis arose. Do you have photos from that time? If so, take a look at them to remind yourself of your life then. If you were using a planner, calendar, or journal during that time, pull it out and review what was going on for you then. If not, do your best to remember.
2. Write (or type) out answers to the following:

    - What were your key goals in your personal life at that time?
    - What personal challenges were you seeking to solve?
    - What were your key goals in your work life then?
    - What work challenges were you seeking to solve?
    - What were your key goals in your home life then?
    - What domestic challenges were you seeking to solve?

Now consider your current circumstances. What's important to you today?

ACTIVITY

Jot down answers to the following questions:

- What are your current goals and challenges in your personal life?
- What are your current goals and challenges in your work life?
- What are your current goals and challenges in your home life?

Compare your answers in the previous two activities. What priorities remain the same? What has shifted because of your crisis?

It might be that a particular project is no longer so imperative. Or that something that you weren't really interested in before has now become a pressing matter. Perhaps your crisis has heightened your motivation to accomplish a particular goal. Maybe you've been inspired to chart a new course of action.

Next, assess how you weigh different areas of your life today.

ACTIVITY

1. For each of the following areas of life, assess how important it is to you at the moment, using a scale of "0" (completely unimportant) to "10" (vital):

    Health/Fitness _____
    Professional _____
    Domestic/Home Life _____
    Romantic _____
    Social _____
    Spiritual _____
    Financial _____
    Personal Pursuits _____
    Fun/Leisure _____
    Personal Development _____

2. Choose three areas of life that are most important to you. Circle them.

Next consider your future aspirations. What are your hopes and dreams for the future?

As well, contemplate your experiences during your crisis. What have you enjoyed? What have you missed? What do you appreciate differently? Will you spend your time differently, going forward? How will you spend your money in the future?

As you move into the unknown future, how do you want to be living your life?

ACTIVITY

As you look forward to the future:

- What would you like to do more of?
- What would you like to do less of?
- What would you like to learn?

- What skills would you like to acquire or strengthen?
- What new habits and practices would you like to begin?
- What challenges would you like to overcome?
- On what would you like to spend your money?
- What causes would you like to support?
- What dreams would you like to pursue?

Next, think farther ahead. Forget about reality for a moment and imagine how you would like your life to unfold, ideally. Pretend that ten years from now you are living a wonderful life.

ACTIVITY

Imagine that it is ten years from today. A decade has gone by and things have unfolded beautifully. Imagine that you fully enjoy and appreciate your life. You are content, fulfilled and happy.

- Describe your preferred life in as much detail as possible. Involve your senses as much as possible: What are you seeing? What are you hearing? What are you feeling?
- Where are you living? What is your home life like?
- Describe a typical day.
- What has happened in your personal life that has made you pleased and proud?
- What have been the highlights of your work life?
- What do you love about your life?

If you wish, gather your ideas and insights in a journal or folder. Continue to add to it, using the activities in the subsequent sections of this chapter.

◆

TAKE STOCK OF YOUR PERSONAL RESOURCES AND LIABILITIES

You are not entering the uncertain future empty-handed. You are a competent person who has handled everything in your life thus far. Whatever happens, you have your skills, talents, strengths, and knowledge at your disposal. In times like this, it's helpful to remind yourself of your personal resources.

ACTIVITY

Please write or type your answers to the following questions:

- What are your personal strengths? What do you like best about yourself?
- For what do you receive the most compliments?
- List your skills and talents.
- List your key areas of knowledge.
- Which of your personal qualities have been particularly helpful during your crisis?

These personal strengths have helped you the past. They can help you now and in the future. For example, if you are a creative person, you might be adept at developing innovative solutions to challenges. It might be that you are turning to artistic pursuits to cope with your crisis. It could be that your inventiveness will generate novel endeavors as new opportunities unfold in the future.

Take a few moments to think about your responses to your crisis. How have you applied your personal resources to what you have been going through?

How else could utilize them in your current circumstances? How might you implement them in the future?

ACTIVITY

Select one of your personal strengths. With it in mind, answer the following questions:

- How has this helped you in the past? Give some specific examples.
- To what extent have you applied it to your crisis? How has it helped you?
- How else might you use this in your current situation?
- How might you apply it to whatever you experience in the future?

As well, contemplate whatever tangible resources you are likely to have available to you. Consider financial assets and things you own as well as personal connections and other possible sources of support.

ACTIVITY

1. What resources, assets, and sources of support are available to you now? Make a list.
2. What might be available to you in the future?

You've got a lot at your disposal to help you navigate the future. Alas, you also have some liabilities. Human beings are fallible. We all have weaknesses, quirks, and foibles. We can be our own worst enemy sometimes, planting self-doubt or sabotaging our success or otherwise impairing us.

However, to the extent that you are aware of your less helpful features, you can mitigate their effects, going forward.

ACTIVITY

Please write or type your answers to the following questions:

- What do you like least about yourself? What are your personal weaknesses?

- What complaints do you hear about yourself from others?
- How do you tend to get in your own way? How have you sabotaged yourself in the past?
- Which of your personal qualities have been unhelpful during your crisis?

Consider how these liabilities affect you.

For example, if you are a worrier, you may tend to stress out yourself and others, fearing things out of your control. Your anxiety might produce a physical reaction and mental strain. Maybe it has caused you to avoid taking risks in the past. It might make decision making difficult because you're afraid of making the "wrong" choice. Perhaps your tendency to worry has escalated into full-blown anxiety during your crisis. It might hinder your ability to take advantage of new opportunities in the future.

Remind yourself of how you have mitigated this liability in the past. What has worked well for you to reduce, control, or overcome it?

For example, if you are a worrier, how have you lessened your fear when it has flared up? How do you calm yourself? What can you do now and in the future to lessen or control your worry?

Remind yourself of how you'd like to be operating as you move into the future.

ACTIVITY

Select one of your personal liabilities. With it in mind, answer the following questions:

- How has this liability hindered you in the past? Give some specific examples.
- How have you moderated or overcome this liability in the past?

- To what extent has this liability affected you during your crisis? How has it hampered you?
- What can you do to address, alleviate, or lessen this liability, now and in the future?

◆

MAKE CONSCIOUS CHOICES

A significant gift of any crisis is that it gives us an opportunity to make deliberate decisions about how we want to be living our lives.

Pause. Think about your life. Consider:

- What you've observed and learned during your crisis
- Your values
- Your priorities and aspirations
- Your personal resources and liabilities

Going forward, how do you want to be living your life? Think about the big picture as well as the details.

Consider specific situations you are likely to encounter (e.g., working, socializing, taking care of your household—whatever scenarios are relevant to you). Consider the specific changes you have already chosen to make, or have found it necessary to make, as a result of your crisis. Which of these adaptations are likely to become permanent? What other modifications might you foresee?

ACTIVITY

1. Clear some time to contemplate your future. Journal about your expectations, hopes, desires, priorities, and intentions as you head into the future.

- What is important to you?
- What do you want to keep foremost in your mind, going forward?
- How do you want to be living your life?

2. Reflect on different areas of life. For each, list changes you've made as a result of your crisis. Circle those that you will continue in the future. Journal about other modifications you are likely to make, going forward. What's important to you? Consider situations you are likely to experience, including:

   - At home
   - At work
   - In likely social situations

Let these insights guide your future plans, actions, and decisions.

You can't control the crises that arise in your life. You can, however, manage your reactions to what is unfolding. When crises occur, it's important to tend to your basic needs first—safety, self-care, physical, mental, spiritual, and social (Chapter 2). Part of this involves handling your emotions (Chapter 3) and managing your mind (Chapter 4). Perhaps the most effective way to cope with a crisis is to take action (Chapter 5). No matter the nature of the crisis, there are always opportunities and unforeseen gifts. It is possible—and beneficial—to take steps to make the best of the situation (Chapter 6). If the crisis is ongoing or long-term, the techniques and strategies in this book are even more valuable (Chapter 7). To prepare for an unknown future, you can rely on your values as well as your knowledge of your personal resources and liabilities to make conscious choices going forward (Chapter 8).

ACKNOWLEDGEMENTS

Thank you to everyone who shared their coping stories for this book.

Sincere thanks to Joan Moffatt Biddie, Janna Stewart, and Nancy Tanemura for reading early drafts of this book. Your comments and suggestions for improvement are much appreciated.

In gratitude for many blessings, a portion of the proceeds of this book is being donated to charity.